SHALONDA CRAWFORD

# Employ Your Pain

*Putting the Hurt to Work for You*

This book was professionally typeset on Reedsy.
Find out more at reedsy.com

"Every experience is preparation for an experience to come."

Dr. Shalonda K. Crawford

# Contents

# Acknowledgments

To My Husband, Pastor Shep

My PROVIDER. 🖤

- For me and our children: financial, moral, emotional, mental to the very best of your ability.

My PROTECTOR. 🔫🗡

- In EVERY way. Don't believe me? Please don't try me! Intentionally keeping us covered by the Blood. I am perfectly safe. †

My CHEERLEADER. 📣

- The biggest, first and most solid-unwavering support in every prosperous endeavor.

My WATCHER. 👁

- Highlights my blind spots so that I may shine in my very best light. Never left in the shadows.

My KING. 👑

- Keeps me Queening at all times. I am at your side and there is absolutely no other place I'd rather be.

The words "Thank You" fail to express the sentiments of my heart and the depth of your rock-solid and resolute support, provision and protection of me and our family. You are nothing short of an exemplary husband-leader. Your verbs in our union only example the wonderful and consummate nature of who you are. You have shown up as my chief advocate and soldier of valor on the front lines of every productive effort that I have chosen to endeavor. You are seen, recognized and appreciated.

### To My Children
Brandin Sr., Nicholas, Lauryn, Kinnidi, Madisyn, Malachi and grandson, Brandin Jr.

Each of you are your own precious and illuminous jewel in my crown. I am deeply grateful for your places in my heart and life. You have drawn the very best of me even as you shine all on your own. You have allowed me to experience tenderness at a depth unimaginable and before you, unfathomable. Your mother's love is forever unwavering. I am fully alive inside of my tribe!

### To My Parents
Mom, from the bottom of my heart I will always appreciate all of the sacrifices that you made especially and specifically for me. I'm extending a very special thanks to you for doing the best you could with what you had, when so many times you had so little. From you, I have successfully learned the life skill of making a dollar out of fifteen cents. It wasn't tough love. It was tough times and hardcore love. I am eternally grateful.

Dad, for as long as I can remember, you have always encouraged and believed in me. You planted seeds in the deepest parts of me and left me with the tools that I have needed to meritoriously cultivate them. This book project is just one of the many harvests that have blossomed to fruition. For so many of our early years I was reluctant to open up and embrace you. I was unable to appreciate you. But no worries. I hear you loud and clear now. I'm doing my best dad, and I can only hope that you are proud. May you rest in peace. (May 20, 1955 – December 7, 2012)

## To My Gramma Jessie

You mean the world to me. As I observe the depths and richness of your life, I am inspired in so many ways. I have been nothing short of blessed to have a person in my life with such a huge, loving, giving, humorous, and open heart. Thank you for not only showing up in some of my clutch seasons but in many instances, for actually being the clutch! (that'll go over some heads) I only wish to follow in your footsteps. You are my sunshine.

## To My Sissy Tori

You are my personal puzzler. Thank you for picking up all of my scattered and fragmented pieces and putting me back together again. And again. And again. And yet again.

## To ECM, My Friends, Family, and Community

To my ECM Fam - IYKYK! I can feel the wind on my face. You are the wind beneath my wings. Because of you I am free to jump out of the box and yet stay grounded in God's Word. Having solid family, friends, church and community circles keep me motivated to going on and soar. Many thanks to each of you.

Robin, you are not often seen but present. Your prayers, spiritual covering, listening ear and sound counsel are invaluable.

And to my Day 1'er-Stunnas, Bernita & Janell – Because of you I know what TRUE friendship looks like. I OVERSTAND what true friendship feels like. You are my rocks. Thanks for staying in the ring and fighting these battles with me. In real life we've been down like 4 flat tires, 4 decades in... I'm pretty sure there are more battles to come!

# Prologue

### Lying Ears
*A Letter to Myself*

Dear Shalonda,

Quiet the pain please.

Do you remember when that woman told you that, "*Your presence is too loud when you enter the room?*" Girl! She didn't know. Freedom was still new to you. She had no way of knowing that your freedom was only a few years behind you. Though you had a lot to say, you hadn't taken the liberty to share with her. Not yet. She didn't realize how long you'd been silenced, muted. You had so much to share but . . . she could not have known how many times you screamed from the top of your lungs to be heard and still nothing came out. Shame, shame, shame. How could she know?

You are just Carla's daughter. So much to tell but no medium to release it. Shalonda, you are just Gary's daughter too. So much seen and witnessed but only preempted stages and venues to reenact it out on. Have you been pretending, Shalonda? Had that woman infiltrated your act? Does she see beyond the mask and through your casting?

Well no. She couldn't have. She had no vantage point from which she could have imagined you jumping up and down, doing head spins, and flipping cartwheels to be seen, noticed, recognized, acknowledged. Nah. I would beg to differ. You had your world bamboozled, right? How could she know?

Time had gone by since that day when the memory chanced on you. *"Too loud,"* she said. Almost as if out of the blue, it was days later when you pondered what she may have meant by *loud.* How is presence loud? You literally had not yet mustered a single word when you silently trumpeted into her office. Don't you recall being in quite a good mood?

There it is! Perhaps it's your good mood that masks and blares. Perhaps it was your seeming smile that matched your disposition. Shalonda, be honest. Haven't you fooled most? Of course you have. Be careful girl. Your windshield is foggy. Being terribly afraid of people rejecting the parts of you that you won't allow them to see has always clouded your point of view. Down through the years, you've really perfected the act. Let's be real. You've got the Dr. Sunshine thing down to a T!

Ahhhhh . . . that's it! Dr. Sunshine is loud. Is Shalonda really Dr. Sunshine or the other way around? Who's the loud one, you or her? Who's the polished imposter? Is it her or is she you? I'm confused. Understandably so. But don't *you* be fooled. There is a good chance that your world is as oblivious as I am. There have been so many moments in your life that foreshadowed with clarity just how much easier it is to *accept it* than it is to be *accepted.*

But when I squint my eyes and narrow my focus, I can plainly see. It is the shield of Shalonda's deafening silence that she hides behind the sunshine.

And just like that woman, no one saw what everyone heard.

With Love & Concern,
Shalonda

# Introduction

*"Effie, We All Got Pain..."*

Though my life has already rendered *countless* peaks and victories and celebratory moments, I too, like you, have my ongoing portion of suffering. I was introduced to pain at a very young age. I am not referring to the pain that is felt as discomfort to our physical bodies. No. Not the pain that leaves behind skin scabs and scars to mark experiences as evidence of their past existence. I am referring to the pain that renders mental torment, jarring flashbacks, shame, guilt, and memories that are rather not visited. I am referring to those experiences that render emotional wounds. I am referring to pain that intrudes upon dreams at night and, if not careful, those dream catchers can be robbers of the dreams of our lives. Some of our painful experiences cut a little or a lot deeper than others. But Effie . . . we ALL got pain.

I am no different from you.

I have experienced the pain of rape, molestation, and domestic violence, the shame and down-casting of being a teenaged mother, battles with self-esteem following *numerous* personal disappointments, failures, insecurities and the sheer inability to meet mine or other's expectations, divorce of my parents, intimate partner betrayals, friend-ship betrayals, family betrayals, ridicule and bullying, surviving and struggling with inadequate basic necessities due to low economic circumstances, and the effects of poverty like inadequate food, clothes, and utilities. I have battled tremendous grief following the death of my brother and then my father and other family members and close friends. I have endured bouts with depression and anxiety in every stage of life, church hurt, informed, and misinformed judgment of others, complex issues due to my late father's and other close acquaintance's struggles with drugs and alcohol, and the list simply goes on and on and on and on and on.

I am no different from you.

Dang, Effie. We all got pain.

# I

# Part I: On Boarding

*"The beginning is always today."*
*–Unknown*

# 1

# The Tree of Life

*"If you feel like you're losing everything, remember that trees lose their leaves every year and they still need to stand tall and wait for better days to come."*

*-Unknown*

You ask, *"Onto what am I coming aboard?"*

Great question. From the moment we exit the womb, we climb aboard the Life Experience. No discrimination. Everyone is invited. Everyone is included. No one is left out; no one escapes it. We each get a different and individually unique version of it, but Life Experience is our one common thread. Life Experience, though inevitably and involuntarily thrust upon us, is not always the simplest to manage and maneuver. Life is not easy and the experience of it all can take time for us to digest, process, grow, and develop. Some master it whizfully and others . . . well, not so much. The common of us struggle to grasp an understanding and appreciation of the valleys of life as opposed to the warm embrace of its opposite peaks.

As branches extending from the Tree of Life sits Joy. Another branch is Pleasure alongside Contentment. There are branches of Advantage, Blessings, and Comfort, as well as that of many other branches. But the one branch that stands out, shunned from all the other popular blossoms, is the branch of Pain. Though Pain impresses the most salient imprint on our minds, consciousness, and worldview, it is the least invited but frequently visited. Furthermore, there is much energy exerted in trying to push Pain out of sight, make it disappear, or cut its branch completely off of the tree all together. But just as all the other branches are extensions of Life Experience that cannot be entirely consumed, so too is the branch of Pain. When cut, it simply bides its time and when least expected, it sprouts right back up. We all have one or a few bouts with Pain. And it's all fair game because no one is left out or at any point, banished from the Tree.

*Making a Money Tree*

You are in possession of a money tree. You have a wealth of experiences stored up inside of you. They are etched in your being. Now, whether or not you capitalize on those experiences is entirely up to you. Each and every experience that you have endured has value. There are no wasted experiences, only opportunities to invest. We must be good stewards and apply wisdom to our experiential investments. Investments can lead to bankruptcy or harvest. There is an old saying that goes, "Money doesn't grow on trees." Well, I would beg to differ. Experiences are like the seeds of the Tree of Life.

As for the adage, "*Money doesn't grow on trees,*" let's unpack it a bit. In other words, money does not come freely, easily. It implies that money is earned by way of hard work; not easily attained. When you work hard for the money, you are very conscious, smart, and selective about how it leaves your hand. You are careful not to allow hard-earned dividends to willfully fall away from your tree like autumn leaves in the wind.

It is fair to say that we all have the urge or inclination to at least wish our pain away, erase it, or rewrite it. But before you do, allow me to posit that the very branch of pain that we so desperately want relief from, may be our best pathway to the big payoff. Here's the catch. It only pays out when you learn how to best use it as a life investment. If properly attended, the seed of pain can lead to a harvest of dividends that ultimately become the hardest working employee on your team.

Your experiences are valuable, in fact they are invaluable. None of them are worthy of the wayside. The more painful your experience is, the more value there is in your investment. However, there is always a looming risk. The risks of guilt, shame, failure, and judgment are ever-present and continually on the prowl. Nevertheless, as in all investments, the riskier it is to invest in its benefits, the greater the return and reward there is to reap.

Let us sow.

# 2

# The Intention of Pain

*"Pain serves a purpose. Without it you are in danger. What you cannot feel, you cannot take care of."*

-Rebecca Solnit

P ain is a gatekeeper. A security guard. Pain serves a useful and important purpose. The intention of pain is to prevent and warn us from becoming more injured. Its discomfort is the psyche screaming out to alleviate the present pain and to prevent any undo future pain. Pain shows up to open our closed eyes. As counter-intuitive as it may seem, pain has a necessary and intentional place in our lives. All of it. Psychological, mental, spiritual, emotional, physical, all forms of it serve with purpose. Depending on the person and circumstance, they all have different intentions but yet all with the same goal of teaching, preparing, and signaling. Pain is the warning signal. It serves to inform us that something is wrong, out of sorts, not in sync, or off balance. Something has gone terribly awry, and pain is the mail person that delivers the message.

As hurtful as those experiences and lessons may and will be, once that message is received and welcomed with open arms, wonderful things can occur. It is not comfort, but pain that is often the catalyst for personal growth and development. For example, we exercise and lift weights to build muscle and tone our bodies. Naturally, we expect to experience muscle soreness and discomfort. We typically invite it because it signals that our muscles are being challenged to grow and develop as we workout. The muscle becomes stronger and even more resilient.

Now say, for instance, we are trying to learn and master the new skill of learning an instrument. As a beginner, hitting the notes right and capturing a good pitch can be frustrating, but every great musician increases in patience and confidence, develops the craft, and endures the process. Mental and psychological pain work the same way. We develop headaches when we are stressed or overwhelmed with anxiety. It is our gatekeeper informing us that we need to employ some form of self-care. Those are the types of incidents that cause us to deeply reflect on what is important and valuable. Pain makes us aware of the need to make changes that lead us to be more insightful and self-aware.

Pain is a necessary agent in healing and transformation. When we metaphorically place pain on the table, look at it, and deal with it face on, we can then begin to heal beyond the wound that was caused, resolve the inner hurt, and live life at a deeper and more purposeful level. It is at that deeper and more purposeful level that pain becomes a connector. Because pain is what we all have in common, it can serve as a conduit that connects us to others who have similar lived experiences. Lived experience is the seat that fosters empathy, compassion, and collective humanity. Stop and think for a few moments.

Have you ever been motivated to do differently or think differently in response to a painful experience? I believe that I am a better friend to those that are in my circle of life today as a result of having several dear friendships come to unexpected ends. Some of those relationships ended by actions and fault of my own, others not so much. At varying levels and depths, they were hurtful, nonetheless. Painful experiences are often at the helm of our most productive life changes, advanced maturity and the facilitator for improved perspectives.

The intention of pain is to sound the whistle and alert you. The intention of this book is that you no longer exert effort silencing the whistle blower that is you. From today forward you have a new assignment. Sound off! Let pain work its purpose.

# 3

# Pain

*"No test is worth anything unless it's tough to pass."*

-*Dr. Shalonda Crawford*

*I just wanna love the Lord and sing...*

The protective ways that the human brain can blur memory has always intrigued me. It was sometime around the summer of 1995, or maybe it was '94. I'm not sure. It was the summer before the blizzard hit New York City.

For as far back as I can remember, even as a very young girl, I dreamt of being a big-time singer. I sang for my family in the living room, then at family reunions. I even got a few solos in my uncle's children's choir. I just wanted to sing. My father was a saxophonist who could see the stars in my eyes. He pushed me. In retrospect, he may have been pushing me harder toward his own dreams than my own, but he pushed and supported me, nonetheless. He entered me in talent shows, karaoke competitions, and I eventually became the lead singer of his band, taking gigs all over the city.

At some point, my talents caught the attention of a known music manager in New York City. Together, we embarked on several music deals and opportunities with a few major studios and record labels. All with no avail, until one independent gospel record executive caught wind of my demo. Gospel. Gospel? Not exactly what I had in mind but, okay.. . I really do love the Lord with all of my heart. So . . . maybe. After all, church and pastors were all around me growing up. Both grandfathers were pastors, my uncle was a pastor too. We deeply believed in God, but we rarely attended church, with the exception of special holidays like Easter, as I was tagged along with devout relatives.

Not gospel, but an array of good ole fashioned R&B and jazz swooned in regular rotation at my house. The best of the 70's & 80's pop and soulful R&B bumped on the radio. I loved music, all kinds of music. Still do. I wanted in. But I'd never envisioned myself as a gospel artist. The opportunity was good, and the interest was high. Soon, I began to sign on to the idea. A gospel artist. I hadn't signed on to the label just yet though. Instead, the record company tasked me to begin the work on the album and to perform at venues in a few local and neighboring states before moving forward with the negotiations. Exciting. They linked me up with a few producers and writers in New Jersey and New York and also one writer-producer in my hometown. A gospel artist. At that point I was sold.

*Until I wasn't.*

# 4

# Pain + Passion = Purpose

*"Hurtful experiences can be turned into deepening devices."*

-Dr. Shalonda Crawford

A life without purpose is one that is unfulfilled. At the core of a person is an innate desire for meaning and direction, a sense that as the days fall into the next, there is something to contribute that is bigger than the singleness of self. At our least, there is a yearning to manifest more than what already exists. As we venture into that innate calling, there are a couple of principles that are undoubtedly at play.

*Passion*

It's kinda weird. Strange how our painful experiences are more influential in our memories and in how they shape us than the celebratory ones. Even when we think back, reminisce, and talk about them, special times draw loving smiles, fond and heartfelt memories, a chuckle or

15

laugh. But there is something about pain, that causes compound and complex emotions. As they often show up uninvited, sometimes those memories are so disturbing and disconcerting that they cause rebellion with a vengeance to rise up on the inside of us to fight back and conquer. The overarching gumption is that pain will not prevail.

Why? Because it is the pain in our lives, not the pleasure that fuels passion. It is the passion that burns within us that births advocates, activists, and volunteers of change. Passion born of pain incites us to do what is within our reach and capability to prevent others from facing our challenges alone and moreover, from being buried alive beneath them. We breathe deeper as those whom we assist find their breath. Eventually, our passions become personal missions. Personal missions are the catalysts for divine change and purpose if we allow God to lead us.

Going through the difficult challenges of our existence and coming out on the victorious side of it causes a deeper, more enriched appreciation for life. It is when we become the person that we needed during our times of despair, unrest, and longing that we discover the newfound joys and richness that is ultimately the big payoff. In short, while the shortcomings, blunders, and disappointments can be strenuous, tough, and difficult to endure, they can also very well be the launching pad for personal growth and newfound life purpose.

*Purpose*

What is my God-given purpose? It's a great question. At some point we've all asked it. Well honestly, I don't know and won't pretend to. Like any creation, to find the answer to its intended functionality, we must turn to the original creator. In this case, to know why we were created, we must turn to our Creator. Going about it on our own may yield results, but our efforts pummel in comparison to His. Outside of God's divine Will, we may make a little progress and realize a little success. But more often, we find ourselves constantly crashing against a glass ceiling with no clue how to move beyond it.

Let's take a wrench for example. We can use a wrench to bust the windows out of a car. But that is not what the wrench was created or intended to do. Demolition was not a part of the original plan for the wrench. The wielder of that tool may find success on that destructive mission, and yet we all know that the original creator of the wrench had an entirely different purpose for it in mind. The veracious purpose of anything is watered down or ineffective when not utilized in its proper way.

Don't seek to find the answer to the question, *"What am I to do?"* before seeking the answer to *"Who am I?"* You are an answer. There is someone somewhere praying for a person just like you to enter their life and help them find the light of day, the solution to the pain, and the relief from their grievous reality. Are you in position, ready and up for the call? Someone is praying for *your* help. Are you willing to be discovered?

Pain, if for no other reason, equips your life with great depth and meaning. In spite of all the troubles that we have travailed, we are still rich with abundance, fulfillment, and direction. There is a wealth of purpose that awaits you and those that you are assigned to. Many of us are bankrupt because we do not have the combination to unlock the wealth that is held up for us. The key is in our commitment and service to others.

So, what is my purpose? Though we must seek God for that specific answer, the biggest hint is tucked away inside of our biggest pains. Purpose is not a job. A job or occupation is but one way we walk out purpose. They are vehicles that chauffeur or drive purpose. People who are passionate about the assignment will work from either a position of divine purpose or from a void-stain caused by pain.

*Be a Good Steward*

When we are purpose-driven, we are also good stewards over the experiences that we have endured. We often refer to stewardship in reference to finance. Financial wealth is important. Nevertheless, it is equally important to be a good steward and agent over our experiences as well. All of them; good, bad, and indifferent. Remember, they all have value, significance, and purpose.

It has not always been the case, but at this point in my life, I am personally willing to share any experience that I have ever endured. I no longer bear shame or guilt. I am not proud of every experience, but I also am no longer ashamed of myself for my past. I do not blame myself for what others decided to do or carry their guilt. At the same time, I have not lived a life only on the recipient's side of misfortunes. There are things that I am also guilty of myself like lying, stealing, cheating, betrayals, and such. The worst of my actions, inactions, or victimizations do not define me as the sum of my total being but are valuable facets of it.

That being the fact, I am also not willing to share them randomly or inconsequentially with any and everyone for the sake of a good or entertaining story. I am cognizant of my duty to be a good steward over my experiences, and, by doing so, I am careful to share with pensiveness, diligence, and responsibility. Many of my experiences are highlighted throughout this book. Many others are reserved for more intimate settings, instances, and occasions. This is my real life. I am blessed to have it. I will not arbitrarily allow anyone to exploit any aspect of it haphazardly or intentionally. I will share readily but with the guidance of well-earned wisdom.

## Purpose Paid Forward: It's All About Me

What is paying it forward? The short answer is that it's not about you. But it's all about you. Has anyone ever made you feel really good on the inside? So much so that it left a lasting and positive impression on you? Paying it forward describes the beneficiary of a good deed, repaying that same sentiment of kindness to another or others rather than paying it back to the original benefactor. Put another way, paying it forward is taking in generosity that has been given to us at any point in our lives and spreading it throughout our lives to others.

On a grander scale, Pastor Rick Warren summed it up well in the Day 1 paragraph of his best-selling book, *The Purpose Driven Life*[1]. "It's not about you." The first time I read that line I was jarred. I must have reread that line a thousand times and now I have it memorized, etched on the front of my mind. Reflecting deeper, if I am willing to buy into the pay it forward way of achieving self-fulfillment, then the statement, 'It's not about you' becomes true. It is not about me but all at the same, it's all about me. You may be asking, "How does me helping others benefit me?"

Sharing our gifts and divine purpose to the world is one of the most selfless-selfish acts we can participate in. Believe it or not, our own abilities to heal from everything that life has thrown and will throw at us is wrapped up inside of our willingness to use our experiential wisdom and firsthand knowledge to help heal others. If we do this thing right, we will unlock and release a power so great that the return back to us will be innumerable wealth. Not necessarily wealth in the form of tangible cash or social status but wealth in the form of a charitable contribution that ripples throughout the world. Each time we utilize our capabilities to heal others, we are actively partaking in world change and healing, even if it is as marginal as just one person at a time.

Put another way, if we are agreeable, we will be able to use every one of our hurtful, unfortunate, and traumatic experiences coupled with our joys and successful triumphs to help people who can relate because of similar, direct, or by proxy experiences themselves. Because of the similarity, we will note an unspoken connection and an ability to genuinely have a heart for them. The common and specific pain is the conduit to healing for both you and the recipient. However, a conduit can only be an effective connector if the line is open and clear from your heart to theirs. The more honest and transparent we can be, the stronger the connection can be as well.

Find someone to INVEST in and make a point to continue habitually investing throughout your lifetime. Good investments yield good returns. It is not until we invest that we can expect a return. You have to deposit something in to get something out. There are no dividends, no interest, or any return without investments. No planting, no harvest. Simple. Point blank.

Begin by reflecting on what you have learned and how you have grown from it. We are all survivors. We have all conquered and therefore we are all conquerors. Which experiences display your resilience? I have found that the most painful, shameful, and guilt-ridden experiences have proven the most impactful in assisting others who are going through a rough time and even moreover, when I have found my way to a victorious place. The phrase, "been through the fire, but don't even smell like smoke," describes it well. Any challenge overcome by victory inspires determination and motivation for those who are presently and comparatively struggling.

If we are willing, our pains ignite passion and our passion beckons divine purpose. We are already equipped for the job. It's up to us to accept the offer of assignment.

# II

# Part II: Pre-Qualification

*"The champion for the evening, and the companion for life,*
*require different qualifications."*
*−Samuel Richardson*

# 5

# Trauma

*"The worst day of your life is still filled with potential."*

-Dr. Shalonda Crawford

One of the things that has bothered me quite a bit over the years but particularly as a mental health professional, is how people label or judge what is and what is not "traumatic." Can we just pause for a moment to normalize and set the record straight? Trauma and the way we view and experience it, not just *can* be but actually *is* on a continuum. There is a spectrum. There is a subjective scale that we have to take into consideration. It is not black and white. Like every emotion that involves the human experience, the way we experience trauma in our *individual* lives is like an array of various hues of gray.

For clarity, trauma is not in and of itself a diagnosis. Trauma describes an inner experience. In the book, The Myth of Normal: Trauma, Illness & Healing in a Toxic Culture[2] , Gabor and Daniel Mate explain, "Trauma is not what happens to you . . . it is what happens *inside* you as a result

23

of what happened *to* you."

I have chosen not to dive too deep into definitions, but a few may be helpful. There are essentially three types of traumas and one mass machine. They are acute, chronic, complex, and systemic traumas. I will be brief.

Acute trauma typically results from a single and isolated incident, like a physical altercation, a serious injury, or a car accident. Chronic trauma typically happens when the event is repeated and prolonged like, homelessness, domestic violence, or chronic illnesses. And then there is complex trauma, which is exposure to varied and multiple traumatic events, usually of an invasive and/or interpersonal nature. For example, ongoing neglect or abandonment, physical or sexual abuse or incest, human trafficking, events that are of a more severe and of an ongoing nature like that.

*Making Lemonade*

I'll give you a personal example. As did many of my Black counterparts as children, I grew up in a low-income household. My family was also the only Black family in an all-White middle-class neighborhood. It was God's favor shone through the generosity of our landlord that we were afforded rent at a percentage of the value. Nevertheless, even in its subtlety, my younger brother and I could not escape the reality of racism that came as a stowaway add-on in the package. For the most part, the racism and discriminatory jabs were never blatant but always sneaky. I felt it just beneath the surface, much better than I could articulate with words. The microaggressions underlying many of the ill-intentioned commentary of my White peers and their parents were always written in invisible ink and read between the lines. The gravity of comparison, though impossible to label at that young age, was ever-present. I was then, and am now, very clear that my story of partial means is by no account unique. As an adult looking back, I believe that my family was not the worst off by far, but low-income and being a minority outlier did have an impact and influence that undeniably shaped of my worldview. In many ways those lived experiences, as well as many others, were bricks in my chronic trauma backpack. Still today, I am reminded of their weight every time my senses rise up as I enter a room as the only minority with all White occupants. It rises up when my White counterparts question my capabilities and credentials. Those bricks are in there. My guards are not always visible upon first impression, but the right prompting will call the gloves out of hiding.

I have to admit, it doesn't always serve me well. Over the course of time, I have chosen to reinvest my negative experiences to bank positive outcomes. At the least, I have a pragmatic gain of empathy that cannot be taught but only acquired through lived experience. I intimately understand and now have language for describing, labeling, educating, and calling out racial microaggressions utilizing the empathy I have also attained by way of those very same hurtful experiences. My early childhood exposure equipped me. Today, at the butt of a seemingly innocent racially inspired joke, I may, with a straight face, simply retort with an equally backhanded challenge, "I don't get it." And, when discovered that there is no non-offensive way to explain, the result is typically and effectively a speed course in Racial Microaggressions 101.

Is sameness better than difference? Is belonging worth having if it comes at the cost of your authentic identity? Difference as a child can be debilitating. If we're honest, it's hard to boldly stand apart, especially when we're children. As growing children and young adults, we want so much to fit in and to belong. Being the only minority in many childhood settings forced me into the choice of either sinking beneath the significance of who I inherently am or boldly embrace it. Not immediately but eventually, I learned that there is power and beauty in my Black difference. Furthermore, from my acute and chronically traumatic childhood, I mastered how to stand in a room of "others" comfortably, confidently, and loudly in my born skin.

Exposure to trauma can influence our worldview. As a therapist, I am well aware of how nuances and worldview diversely affect the way some may ingest and perceive experiences like mine. Because trauma is consumed on a subjective spectrum, how you interpret, relate, and respond to the same set of circumstances for yourself may very well present differently on the trauma spectrum for someone else. The younger we are at the time of the adverse event, the greater the probability of embracing a negative worldview and maladaptive methods of psychological and practical survival strategies and tactics. To add, as a not-so-shocking reality, let's highlight the fact that research widely shows that children are particularly more vulnerable to the effects of trauma, primarily because they are exposed before having developed any strategies for defense. The National Child Traumatic Stress Network[3] notes that, "young children are less able to anticipate danger or to know how to keep themselves safe, and so are particularly vulnerable to the effects of exposure to trauma."

Furthermore, during traumatic experiences, the brain goes into a heightened state of stress and fear-related hormones are activated. And although stress is a normal part of life that we all navigate to various degrees, when a child is exposed to chronic trauma, the brain remains in that elevated and hyper-sensitive, vigilant, and defensive-protective pattern. Elongation causes many children to grow up into adults with thinking, perspectives, and mindsets that are rooted in subconscious stress, which weigh on emotional, behavioral, and cognitive functioning. As a result of that continued stress, they unknowingly live their lives on constant survival mode. For them, the everyday norm is fight or flight.

It was in my own therapy sessions that I learned that the root cause of my emotional and psychological fragility around my basic support is based in the awareness of my need to subsist as a child. While children in secure homes are tasked and focused on developmentally thriving, me and others like me are consumed merely with surviving. I discovered that even as a person who is blessed with the safety of financial stability, secure relationships, food, clothing, and shelter, today I am still in a psychological war and fighting a subconscious inner battle with the knowingness and thus present fear of what it means to live with low to no means. Having an explanation and the language to describe our own experiences should either bring some of us to a place of relief and comfort or compassion and empathy for someone else who may have suffered trauma or dysfunction in their early childhood years.

Lastly, there is also systemic trauma. Without going too far into a stratospheric explanation, I want to highlight and acknowledge that for Black people in America there is systemic, societal, and racial trauma that has been perpetually and continuously passed down generation after generation, due to the historic atrocities, injustices, and oppressive forces endured simply for being born Black in this country for centuries now. And it all goes back to the plantation. As a collective, Black people have had to face, adjust, endure, and overcome *a lot!*

To put it mildly, for some, the struggle to get up and make it from day to day is noteworthy in and of itself. For others, the morning commute from the bed to the front door may be a bit easier. It's a spectrum. It looks different for each of us depending on which hand life has dealt and the lens of which we view it from. Many of us are still trying to sweeten the lemons in the lemonade.

27

# 6

# Good Grief

*"Pain from grief is a direct reflection of the depth of love. That's why it hurts so bad."*

-Dr. Shalonda Crawford

The propensity to grieve pain is in direct correlation with the depth of the ability to love. Both may run vast and deep. That is why love feels so good and loss hurts so bad. The depth of the void directly reflects the depth of the love. While grief is profoundly personal and, in many ways, subjective, it is also intrinsically woven into the fabric of life. Grief is the natural response to loss, and, though at times it can hurt very deeply, it can also have some unexpected benefits in its process of healing, recovery, and personal growth.

*Processing.* In therapy, the term 'processing' refers to the method of focusing, digesting, and integrating a person's thoughts, feelings, and experiences in response to an event. Processing often involves directly addressing complicated and traumatic experiences in a very subjective and nonjudgmental way. Loss often brings on feelings of guilt, anger, sadness, and regret among others. Grief works as an outlet for emotional release and expression. Allowing mental and emotional space to fully express true and authentic feelings associated with the void of the loss can initiate the gradual healing work that we need to move in the direction of acknowledgment that opens the pathway to acceptance.

Many of us are familiar with the acronym DABDA to describe the stages of grief. **DABDA** stands for *Denial, Anger, Bargaining, Depression, and Acceptance.* I'll briefly review each.

**Denial** is the mind's way of escaping the reality of the loss. Even when we know logically that the loss has in fact occurred, the heart has a tough time believing that which was lost will not return.

**Anger** is not only very common, but a very normal part of the process. Death can seem cruel or unfair, particularly when we feel like the person passed away before their time. Sometimes we may even become angry with ourselves for what we did or did not get to say or do before the passing and/or loss.

**Bargaining** is often an attempt at making deals or negotiating with God. When we experience the gut-wrenching pain after losing a loved one, sometimes it's hard to accept that there is nothing we can do to change the fate that is.

**Depression** is as sad as it seems and what we often expect in the grieving process. We long deeply for what is lost. Life as we knew it has changed and the future may feel uncertain and scary.

The final stage in the grieving process is **Acceptance**. Though grief may ebb and flow for the remainder of our lifetimes, gradually and with due diligence, the pain begins to lighten. I don't know if it's possible to completely 'get over' anyone or anything that is dear to us, but we can learn to live again, find ways to honor them, and keep the memories close. It is widely known that we do not always experience all of the stages of grief or in any particular order. With that in mind, here are 3 tools to employ when managing the stages of grief.

*Resilience.* As daunting as it may be, the challenge of weathering the emotional grief storm brought on by a loss event can eventually increase our capacity to navigate and prepare for future life strains and setbacks. It is tough work, but trekking the terrain of the process can help build up resilience and coping skills.

*Perspective.* Losing someone or something near and dear to you can shift your perspective and prompt you to rethink your morals, ethics, and values. More importantly, loss can incite personal growth and self-awareness that leads to reprioritizing the importance of relationships, goals, and overall life meaning. In this way, the loss event helps you appreciate the here and now with the most important people in your life. A shift in perspective may be just what is needed to nurture a sense of gratitude and focus on what truly matters to you.

*Acceptance.* The ultimate goal of the grief process is to arrive at healing, wholeness, renewal, and acceptance of the loss. Though the void of losing may never completely disappear, we can forever cherish the thoughts, experiences, and memories that were created. The overarching goal is for the fond memories to remain without the heartache and pain. Understandably, the grieving process is different for everyone as is the circumstances and depth of the loss. Therefore, the benefits of grief may also widely vary from person to person. That stated, there is still a degree of struggle coupled with all levels of hurt. To further manage, here are just a few ways to navigate the grief process.

*Ways to Cope During a Season of Grief*

- *Healing happens in community.* Isolation is detrimental in seasons of grief. Idle and lonely minds run rampantly on negative loops.

When we are left to our own devices inside of our minds, we are at risk for developing issues of depression and anxiety. Depression often starts with a sad mood in response to a relevant and congruent event but then gradually, slowly, insidiously moves into seasonal or major forms of depression. There is no 'easy' way to cope but one of the better approaches is to remain in the company of the right people for you during that difficult time. The right people are good, loving, and supportive people that you have a safe relationship with and that you trust. As much as possible make a point to get involved with a group and stay in the company of your family, mentors, a social network, church, etc.

- *Volunteering has a boomerang effect.* There is magic in acts of giving back to a charitable group or person in the very areas where you are in need yourself. As you pour out your charitable service, time and talents with others, gratitude and fulfillment are then inadvertently deposited right back into you. It is like a reciprocal circle. You pour out, it pours back in. It is not by any means easy. But mustering the mental wherewithal to persist and persevere is worth the payoff of contentment in the end.
- *Start a new tradition.* Do something different or new in honor of the person, place, or thing that was lost. Incorporate it at a memorable or significant time or wherever and whenever is best for you.
- *Move something.* Get active. When you are suffering from a loss, being physically, emotionally, socially, and/or mentally stagnant is a kryptonite. Get up and employ some form of exercise. Movement begets the energy for more movement. Have you ever experienced getting too much sleep? If so, you probably also noted that it takes even more effort to get out of bed. Notice how sluggish you are when your feet finally hit the floor. The less you move, the less you have the desire to.

When we grieve we should be mindful to give ourselves the grace needed to make our way through the journey to healing. Allow yourself to fully feel whatever it is you feel in real time. If you want to cry, don't hold it in. Cry. If you think of a fond or funny moment, allow yourself to smile and laugh. Scream if your body calls for it. Allow yourself the freedom to authentically and unapologetically feel. When we use our grievances as activators instead of locking them down and trying to push them away, we are then free to move through the grieving stages and process. We don't simply "get over" grief. With intention we grow through it.

# 7

# The Necessity of Pain

*"Again! You will inevitability repeat the mistakes that you don't learn from."*
                                                                    -Dr. Shalonda Crawford

P ain. Everyone has it and will live with it for life. That's unavoidable. The choice before you is, *"Will you work for the pain or will the pain work for you."* Everyone is living out their pain as either a motivator or a stumbling block. Be it good or bad, it *is* a motivator. Let's take a walk. . . .

- Every January people flock to weight loss programs and gyms with gleeful optimism. They are enthusiastic about losing weight and toning up. In every workout gym, there is an array of instruments to assist their efforts. Knowing that pain is inevitable in order to achieve a fit body, they pay the fee, enter the gym, and choose the instrument of pain based on the area of the body that is most in need. Why? Because it is the necessity of pain that will lead to the desired healthy, slimmer, toned, and fit, body outcome.

· We celebrate the announcement of pregnancies fully knowing that the next 9 months will be uncomfortable for the expectant mother. Still, with an innate and indescribable joy, we endure morning sickness, insatiable cravings, physical discomfort, fatigue, weight gain, and the list goes on. But somehow there is also a fearful excitement when the expectant mother enters the grueling process of labor and delivery. The family is collectively happy about the painful process. So much so, that they begin cheering the Mom on along the way. Why? Because that pain is working to birth a new arrival.

· Parents flock to their pediatric doctors with infants, toddlers, and adolescents in tow to make sure that their children are immunized. Oh, the tears, cries, and sounds of dismay that fill those doctor's rooms and hallways. As much as the children dread the shots and the process of immunization, parents allow it. A child's mind finds it nearly impossible to understand, but the wisdom and life experience of their parents intercede. Why? Because parents and doctors fully understand that the temporary pain of the shot will prevent them from long-term ailments in the future.

In those instances, pain acts as motivation or prevention. But in other circumstances, pain can be a barrier that prevents the most optimal outcome and that pummels down on motivation.

Remember, at the beginning and end of the day, it is not about you. But still, it is all about you, in that your healing is wrapped and bundled inside of your willingness to use your knowledge and experiences to heal others. All of our experiences are of value, not only for us, but for many others that we have the ability to touch and inspire directly and from a distance as well.

# 8

# Post-Traumatic Enlightenment

*"Be realistic about the hurt. Hang on to the lesson."*

-Dr. Shalonda Crawford

## The Power of Enlightenment

E nlightenment is profound insight that undergirds wisdom and thought liberation. Generally speaking, it is depth, understanding, and insight that brings about a sense of clarity and often even inner peace. When we arrive at a place of heightened self-awareness intact, enlightenment is strongly linked to profound personal growth and transformation of self. When things are locked away in the subconscious, trying to push forward toward the enlightenment of the consciousness, healing awaits. Until then, there is something deep-seated that we have an inkling exists but yet feel like we are fighting the wind to find it. Just like the wind, hidden consciousness is a culprit that we know is there but cannot see, locate, identify, and therefore target.

The profound transformation and self-realization that is enlightenment is significant. Enlightenment releases mental slush in an effort to be emotionally available.

More importantly, as antidote for pain, one way to become free from the grip of negative emotions, thoughts, memories, detachments, and deep fears and move toward mental and emotional liberation is through the power of enlightenment. Seeking enlightenment in the areas of life that are most importantly intimate to self is strongly encouraged. When we attain it, we inadvertently inherit higher states of consciousness, authentic joy, harmony, compassion, and unity with self in relation to our internal subjective worldviews and society. Enlightenment is a spiritual awakening. The overall goal in short is to bring about positive change on a personal and idiosyncratic at large level.

*What Doesn't Break You Makes You Qualified*

Whether by firsthand account or by proxy, not everything that happens to you remains bad for you. You are officially an expert in the areas of your life where you have endured and survived trauma and pain. It is not widely discussed, but there are positive psychological changes and effects that can result from your struggle with trauma. Your survival is noteworthy, commendable in fact. Take the time to give credence and credit to yourself for suffering and persisting in whatever you have overcome. Let that sink in.

You have overcome. With that, you now have an important choice to make. You can officially identify as a victim of your circumstances or as a survivor of them. The decision is entirely yours. Which title will you employ? This is not to suggest or make light of the real and often tremendous stress in any way that often accompanies a person's overall well-being following a trauma experience. Post-traumatic stress disorder is no joke and can be a debilitating condition to defeat. Still, trauma *can* enlighten you.

I remember so vividly the night of February 12, 1999. It was 2:48 am when the phone rang. I knew it was bad. It had to be. At that hour, only a tragedy made sense. *Somebody is dead*, I thought. I didn't answer. Instead, I willed it to go away. The phone rang again. I took a deep breath and braced myself for terrible news. His girlfriend's mother was on the other end of the line informing me that my only brother was gone.

"Gone?!" I screamed out to the top of my lungs in agony and utter disbelief. Nothing prepared me. No one told me this was possible. This was a story only made for TV, right? Couldn't be me. Can't be my story. If only I could wake up from this dream. But it wasn't a bad dream. It was a real-life nightmare. The first of its kind in my experience.

It was 9 days from his 24th birthday. My brother's life was snatched by a drunk driver on one unassuming night as he attempted to exit an Atlanta, Georgia, freeway. Gone. Just like that. As the two of them lay on the side of the highway off ramp, he took his last breath in my father's arms. Damn! My very first BFF was no longer here on Earth with me. Immensely, I struggled to navigate the moment. Shortly thereafter, I struggled to navigate life. What is its meaning? What is my purpose? What was his? Why are we even here? What am I going to do now? Can I move on? How? Will I ever heal? How? How will I survive? Oh Lord, this pain. Agony!

From that day, my life was forever changed. To be enlightened is to gain a greater understanding of our world or a more conscious understanding of ourselves. I have discovered that different people have varying ideas about what enlightenment means to them. We can posit then that enlightenment, in general, is subjective to some degree. Nevertheless, we can safely suggest that enlightenment is an emergence from a person's blind obliviousness. Early one fateful morning my brother lost his life. In the wake of it, I set on a mission to make meaning of mine. There was a hidden gain. I had been enlightened to the value and fragility of life. As a result, I had a determined energy to discover purpose that was fueled by painful wisdom. I had heard for as long as I could remember that life is short. Now, I know just how short life can be, how short life is.

I would advise that you learn as much as you possibly can as a sideline observer. It is always better to avoid the fire but get the lesson, than it is to get burned first-hand in the process. Capitalize on the notes taken from others and heed their warnings of looming destruction. Keep in mind, however, that what classroom lectures and YouTube tutorials lack is a catch-all capability. You have paid a heavy price for the unmediated experience that you now possess. If you are not standing upright on top of your game, trauma can zap the things that you value most in life. Moreover, it can cause a secondary injury by adding on a grueling grieving and recovery process. The victim and the survivor are identities left in your hands. Which title will you employ?

# 9

# Faded Faith

*"The way you handle power says a lot about your character."*

-Dr. Shalonda Crawford

*I almost lost my faith. But I didn't.*

My mind worked determinedly to redirect and focus itself. "Just concentrate on the smell. It'll all be over soon." The more I zeroed in on the leg of the steel piano stand, the less connected I was with the moment in real time. I zeroed in on the stand's black plastic knobs. I took particular note of the rubber ends that held the Casio-like keyboard firmly in place. I drifted. Further disconnected from real time. Mmmmm . . . there was chicken frying in the kitchen above me. I love the smell of fried chicken as much as I do the taste. Definitely one of my favorites. But not on this day. In that moment I was paralyzed. As I struggled to maintain focus and concentrate on the soulful aroma, I could not will myself to move out of submission. As I lay there, a disinclined contestant in his game, I was hopelessly hitched to this unsolicited sexual encounter and yet desperately crawling out of my body at the same time.

Again, I redirected, "Lord, this is Your guy, right?"

The confusion suddenly rushed in and hit like a ton of bricks and yet I pondered, "He's a pastor, so is *this*, okay? Is *this* Your will?"

The penetration didn't feel divine, and it certainly didn't feel good. In fact, I had a difficult time feeling much of anything in my physical body or my human–spiritual being. Though there had to be about a million rushes of this-and-that running through my mind and body, I again attempted to redirect my mind in a fraught effort to disconnect it from what was happening between my thighs. My focus moved to the ceiling. It reminded me of my idea of the moon's surface. A muted-dull gray, dimpled, concrete-like surface, with several tiny holes.

As he humped and grinded at an increasingly faster pace, I remained unbendingly focused. From the floor, as I lay halfway under the keyboard stand, the ceiling, or rather the moon, seemed not so far away. This pastor-producer man had taken me riding in his rocket and all of a sudden, BAM! It stopped and I was dropped. Just as fast as it had started, it was over. Uneventful.

Without haste, he jumped up, fastened his pants, and hopped back on the Casio-like keyboard. For about 10 seconds, pants still nestled just beneath my knees, I laid in what seemed a mixed cloud of sorts. I felt confused, betrayed, dismayed, but mostly guilty. In that same instance a mountain of shame and disappointment clothed me. "*How did I let this happen?*" For the next several years I bore the burden of that act. I wore it like a mask. It was my secret identity, and I hid timidly behind it. Trauma.

I was a new Christian. I had just recently joined a church. Because I felt responsible, my prayers changed. My faith faltered. I spent a lot of time fervently apologizing to God about my shortcomings, sins, and that inability to rise in the midst of the salacious occasion. I sincerely believed that I'd failed the "temptation" test. And though I eventually cut ties with the producer-pastor, I lived in fear of God's retaliation, punishment, and condemnation and worked hard to redeem myself of that entire ordeal.

I later learned of the Grace of God and of His perpetual fountain of forgiveness. Thank God for Jesus and the knowledge that faith is built on tests and trials.

Raped by a pastor? I'm certain it is not hard for anyone to understand how my faith in God may have wavered. I went on a deliberate mission to recover it. Along my grieving and healing journey, my faith began to build and restore. With the newfound understanding that free will is always at play and that some acts are outside of God's will, I was relieved to learn that I'd been carrying an unwarranted burden of guilt and shame as I embraced the understanding that none of it was my fault. None of it was my fault. None of it. Much later I'd learn that this pain, like all the others, would hold an opportunity to tap into deep and meaningful life purpose.

Damn, I just wanted to sing.

# III

# Part III: The Hiring Process

*"You will never arrive if you don't know where you're going."*
*-Dr. Shalonda Crawford*

# 10

# Getting On With Life

*"It's not too late to be what you may have been."*

-Dr. Shalonda Crawford

A t the beginning and end of the day, it is all up to you. What you do in the in-between is up to you. With the exception of God, no one in your life is higher than you. Aside from God, no one else has more authority over you than you. Even if you choose to surrender or delegate that authority to someone else, under normal circumstances, that is a choice that you make in the best interest of yourself. Therefore, you are already in the place and position of the Chief Executive Officer (CEO) that is responsible for you. As CEO, once you come of age, you are chiefly in charge of making the major decisions of your company's life, managing its automation and overall operations, upholding the vision, and implementing the strategic directions to achieve it. You are to oversee all directors, investors, and any stakeholders in your life. With the wisdom that life has already afforded you, you are to discern the best private affairs and the best public face.

The people that you choose to be in your innermost circle of life are considered your Board of Directors. These are essentially your closest friends and family, your inner circle. Though your Board cannot ultimately dictate what you do or how you run the business dealings of your life, they do have influential power that may color how you view yourself privately and in the scheme of society. The values and moral compass of your Board should always be taken into account. They should align with yours. Because of this influential power, you should take careful consideration when allowing people to occupy space on your Board of Directors in your inner circle. As the CEO of YOU, you are responsible for 4 chief tasks for your life, hence your company: **envisioning, appointing, equipping, and managing**.

### *Envisioning*

Vision keeps you grounded. Who are you? How do you see you? What are your dreams and inspirations? What do you aspire to do and become? Who and what are your influences, your role models? What are your spiritual and divine anchors? Where are the areas of your life that need strengthening and refining? What will it take to move you to a better you? Who can help you accomplish that?

Contrary to popular belief, the answers to these questions are not necessarily set in stone but a living work in progress. We are constantly in the process of bettering ourselves, finding more optimal approaches to reaching our goals and crystallizing the vision. It is a never-ending process of unraveling, erasing, experiencing, learning, unlearning, and then re-writing your paradox. The perpetual practice of refining who you are as you grow involves a few key elements.

After you are clear about your vision, the next step is mapping out direction. Direction is achieved after establishing the big picture. The big picture is your long-term, overarching vision for your life. The vision is your life's atlas. Direction activates your road map and guides you toward what you ultimately want to accomplish. Your map may encounter several reboots and buffering due to road construction, detours, and unexpected exits, so flexibility is a must. You have to be prepared and even expect to make last-minute and in-the-moment adjustments as curve balls come along the way. As long as you cling tight to the vision for your life, you'll never get too far off course, and you will always be able to return back to the right track.

*It's Never Too Late to Get Back on Track*

During my sophomore year of high school, shortly after turning 15, I found out I was pregnant. Dang. After reemerging from the fog of denial 20 whole weeks later, the weight of the world fell on top of my head. The pressure was enormous, monstrous in fact. Everything that I had worked for up to that moment had passed through my fragile little grip in that very moment. Feeling like a sideline observer, right before my eyes, my train began coasting off of its course.

Panic. I was captain of the volleyball team, a distance runner on the track and field team, a cheerleader, and an honor roll student. What will the principal think of me now? What about my coaches and teammates? Bigger than all of that, what will my parents have to say? What will they do? Little did I know, my life had completely derailed. I just didn't know it yet. My underdeveloped mind was so disconnected from the severity and consequential road ahead, that its narrow-focus was more attuned to the doom of being grounded and put on punishment than the gravity of this life-altering event. It wouldn't take long though. Life showed up. My son was born 12 days before my 16th birthday.

My big picture vision was my saving grace. Yes, I had a child to take care of now. He anchored me. But I also had a small village to help me. I was determined to graduate high school on time right in line with the rest of my class cohort. At that young age, I had not yet pinned down a definite career path, but I knew I wanted to travel and explore the world. I was as clear as I could be at that point in my life with the very limited worldview that I had so far been afforded. I would either be a superstar singer or, as a backup plan, I wanted to work for a big-shot corporation and totally boss a big-time executive position. I had big dreams that left no room for caving under a mountain.

With vision at heart, I persisted. Of course, I weathered a few detours. Okay, *a lot* of detours along the way. Nevertheless, barely but eventually, I walked the stage on time with my graduating class. With a big picture in my back pocket, for now, I was back on track.

The vision is the boss. According to the National Clearinghouse Research Center[4], in 2020, a staggering 39 million young adult people started school but do not finish. Circumstances can only circumvent the big picture if we, as CEO, decide to appoint our circumstances as our replacement at the top. Be sure to remember, never be detoured by the detours. In other words, stay with it. Hard times, changes in plans, and misfortunes will happen. Take the time, fortitude, and resources that you need to, for however long you need to. But then, envision the vision and find your way back.

### *Appointing*

Appointing key and core people in your life to occupy intimate spaces is one of the more crucial decisions you'll make as the CEO of you. These people make up your inner circle and they may also sit on your Board of Directors. Who you allow into the inner circle of your world will help to fuel you and ensure that you are operating a good and sustainable "business" life. The inner-circle folks in your life are the ones who keep you accountable, have your best interest at the forefront, are cheering in your corner, and ultimately want to see you win. The people you place around you are a huge factor in establishing the height of your ceiling.

A handful of those people will be *Determination Advocates* (DAs). DAs will not necessarily be agreeable with you but are in your life to keep you focused on your own vision and to embolden you to see beyond the obstacles immediately in front of you. They may not be the easiest to work with, they may have a history of stirring the pot or working your nerves, but they will keep you dynamic and in your uniqueness. They will advocate for you and to you. They will push you and challenge you to continue to strive beyond any unfortunate situations and circumstances by highlighting your essence and holding up the mantle that pushes you toward your potential. DAs will make their best efforts to hold you accountable to yourself.

Choose wisely, always keeping in mind that the people who are closest to you have the biggest opportunity to influence you negatively or positively. We all love a good cheerleader in our corner, as we should. We need them. They incite us. They have an important seat at the table. But be equally dutiful to also note the people who post up in the corners of your life who are not clapping and celebrating your success and good times. Vigilance is vital.

As CEO, you must be clear about what you're looking for. Take inventory. Know the important positions of your life and staff them. Take the time to think about the traits, values, and morals that are principal to you. Which fundamental characteristics do they possess that are important to you. Though many things can be developed and/or taught, characteristics like trust, loyalty, dependability, reliability, confidence, integrity, and empathy must at least be in there, and if not now, available to further cultivate. Lastly, be mindful of their tolerance for you to be and present your authentic self with them without judgment. Lock in and load up your DAs.

### Equipping

People will treat you the way you equip them to. Equip yourself and equip your team; the people who you have around you. Once you've appointed and secured the right folks in the inner circle of your life and have shared your vision, goals, and dreams with them, you are now ready to move into operation with them. The CEO is the equipper of the organization. You hold the responsibility of cultivating and developing the relationship of your life simply by clearly communicating your vision and your core values. Put another way, share your thoughts, feelings, experiences, opinions, expectations, and views with your folks. When the vision and values are clear, you can release the parental guidance and work along with them autonomously to add their uniqueness to yours and go with the flow.

Remember, you cannot go through life believing that you hold all the cards. You should not be the most knowledgeable person in your life, making all decisions all by yourself, or be in absolute control over everything that goes on in your life. You cannot coexist as the "be-all-end-all" and be successful too. In fact, align yourself with people who have more knowledge, more experience, more resources, skills, and access than you do. There is nowhere to grow if you are already at the top. Let that sink in.

It's a two-way street. The people in your life need to know that you are in their corner and helping to equip them just as much as you want them in yours. You are mutually supplying support and challenge as well. The evidence is the mutual and historical proof of effective results. If you invest your time, deposit your energy, resources, and emotions in the people who align with your vision and goals, they will repay you in many ways and multiple times over as will you for them.

### *Managing*

Considering the fact that we will all experience trauma and pain in our lives, a good CEO will most certainly have to manage a few, if not several, crises. A crisis may be caused by internal (self-inflicted or provoked) factors or external (actions of others or environmental) factors. Life carries with it an enormous range of possibilities and uncertainties. Therefore, it is yet again essential to be equipped and prepared to manage the curve balls of life. How do we do that best?

Mitigation is the gold of management. I am often reminded of an old saying, "The best way to manage a crisis is to avoid one." Of course, even the best among us is not always able to foreshadow when disasters or unfortunate events may strike. Still, simply assuming the inevitable, by creating and settling into a safe space to openly talk about it, can greatly mitigate disaster, sharpen coping skills, and move toward exceptionalism when the worst happens. Do not lose your cool. Be proactive and preemptive. But when things don't go your way or when life isn't lifing as you'd hoped, resist the natural inclination to become reactive.

Ideally, a good CEO exercises cognitive flexibility, acceptance, and preparation as essential mindsets. You will move forward in this life understanding that at various points along the way, reality will kick in. Accept that. When life kicks in, endure. The tides will change if you endure. Resilience separates the survivor from the forfeiter. Bounce back! Take a quick glimpse in the rearview mirror as a reminder of how far you've come and what you've overcome. Things happen, so much as it pertains to you, use your past experiences and observations to prepare for the unexpected. It's important to hone the ability to discern where the next crisis may come from and plan for it.

# 11

# Cargo Pants

*"Healing should be celebrated, not expected."*

-*Dr. Shalonda Crawford*

No matter the color, cargo pants are best known because of their signature utility of having multiple pockets. The pockets are positioned from the top hip waistline, on the sides right down to the very bottom hem of the pant legs. Now, with that said, it may be useful to employ what I call the cargo pants metaphor.

True friendship is quite subjective as it looks differently for everyone. So how friendship is defined or what the expectations are largely depends on the individuals involved. The way you choose to categorize—if you choose to categorize—is perfectly fine if that's what works for you. I understand that I am sharing my personal perspectives and expectations, but if I am honest, even my personal friendship bucket is nuanced at best. I am an unapologetic extrovert and a very outgoing, social person. I consider myself friendly. There are many people that I enjoy interacting with personally, socially, and professionally. However, not all of those relationships are considered equally, though I actually do care for them all. Of course, I feel closer to some than others and I have richer and fonder connections with some as opposed to others. Undoubtedly, you do too.

As we become older, wiser, and grow to experience more interactions with people, we gain a much better understanding of what we want, what we can tolerate, which types of people, things, and social frameworks that we gel with. And so, we inevitably value friendships differently considering how they align. The cargo pants metaphor helps us learn where to place people in our lives. As you have experiences and interactions with people over time, you learn who to place in the hip pockets or side pockets and with cargo pants you know who to position near the bottom pockets at the hem. The more you know, the better you position people in the close inner circles of your life. Others will likely be taken off the pants all together if it is the best decision for your long-term well-being. I have a lot of friends and associates but very few are in my top hip pockets.

# 12

# The Reward of Resilience

*"Falling down is a part of life. Getting back up is living."*

-Dr. Shalonda Crawford

The American Psychological Association (2014)[5] defines resilience as "the process of adapting well in the face of adversity, trauma, tragedy, threats or even significant sources of stress." I was 19 years old. I had a decent job as a receptionist for a small home healthcare agency, making $7.00 per hour. I had a reliable vehicle that I enjoyed driving. And most of all, I had a 3-story townhouse; upstairs, downstairs, and basement. I was fortunate enough to have the blessing and opportunity of a rental subsidy (based on my income) at a whopping $31 a month. The neighbors were friendly. The neighborhood was nice. The commute to work was ideal. Life was good, right?

Two years into this fantasy-like situation, a young White woman with her 4-year-old son moved in next door to me and my then 5-year-old son, and the fantasy began to insidiously unravel. The false allegations and bogus complaints against me began pouring in. On one occasion the police were called to my door in response to a noise complaint. The soft atmospheric jazz that played on the other side of my door was the evidence needed as proof of the absurdity. Needless to say, the police sided with me, and the report was ultimately written in *my* favor. Consequently though, after 3 complaints to the leasing office, the policy stated that I had to be evicted and out in 30 days.

"Wait, what? These accusations aren't even true!" I provided them with the police report as proof of her foolish farce, but to no avail. The policy was the policy. And though they agreed that it should and would be modified, it would unfortunately, not be retroactive for me. The verdict was in and settled. I had to go. The police report did afford me an additional 30 days, but I had to be out by November 1st. Dang.

The room went black. What was I to do now? Where was I to go? How could I afford it? What about my son? Did she think about our welfare and well-being as she was making these complaints? Was this the plan all along? I was staring in the face of adversity, trauma, tragedy, threats, and unbearable stress. Broken, defeated, and unable to rest, I retreated to my basement late that night and through tears I prayed and had a little chat with Jesus. I was confused and just could not understand.

"I'm not wrong. I have not done anything wrong. Lord, how could You let this happen?" The tears rolled mercilessly from my eyes until finally I began professing aloud, *"God, I don't understand but I trust you."* I repeated those very words until I eventually fell asleep. I didn't have answers but I had come to peace.

The next few weeks were tough, particularly as faced with my neighbor's gleeful face and peppy disposition every evening as we both arrived home from work. How could she be so proud of her accomplishment at my demise? Every encounter with her was total and complete torture and drained every ounce of self-control that I could muster not to react. But honestly, figuring out my next move was foremost. Nevertheless, and a long story made short, on October 31$^{st}$, day 59 of the 60 days I'd been given to move out, I signed the deed and moved into my first home. I endured. My resilience was rewarded. Thank God! I passed the test.

When you employ "re" active responding as your norm, you also regress backward toward subconscious and default-protective defenses. It takes time to develop new cognitive pathways in the brain. Pathways are paved over time and by repetition. After each traumatic event, make it a mandatory priority to analyze your new subsequent reality and adjust your mental model to accommodate. Rehearse it in your mind and play it again. Create strong and positive new pathways of resilience to employ moving forward.

Lastly, as a good manager, you'll need to be able to quickly adapt. You can't conquer dreams and achieve vision without being able to stick and move when difference stands in the way and unforeseen circumstances arise. This is life. You've got to roll with the punches or be rolled over.

# IV

# Part IV: The Background Check

*"New beginnings are often disguised as painful endings."*
*–Lao Tzu*

# 13

# The CEO of Me

*"A truly great boss is hard to find, difficult to part with, and impossible to forget."*

-Unknown

First things first, we've got to get our backstories in check. Remember, you are ultimately the CEO of YOU. But are you qualified for the job? When we search your internal history, what will we find? Are you ready to apply for a life promotion? Said another way, are you ready for the next level of life? What are your voids? How and when were they created? How are your past hurts, disappointments, and trauma preventing you from conquering your rightful position? Are they currently hindering you or helping to compete in the Me Against Me competition? Where are your blind spots? Can you locate your areas of limitation? Are you suited for the job of CEO? Or do you need to appoint?

At the start and end of the day—our lives are largely dictated by the decisions we make and the way that we respond to the events and experiences that we encounter and endure. Perspectives, worldviews, biases, and passions are widely shaped and groomed by the lens in which we have experienced life to this point. These lingering questions should be explored and examined before moving further into the personal hiring process. The more healed and whole we are, the more we have maximized our past experiences, the more powerful we can be in the driver's seat of our lives. Let's begin by exploring a few of the things that we may find lingering around and surfacing up in our background checks.

Your dream. Can you see it? Your highest and wildest dream. Can you envision yourself inside of it? Can you imagination it so clearly and so realistically that it can be described precisely in detail? If not, no worries. The lack of vision is just an indication that you have a bit more dreaming to do. I have had so many ideas, plans, and partially developed concepts. Time and time again, my stories ended in failure right at the edge of success. If nothing else, I've learned that there is no route to a dream or any level of subjective success without a vision. I never stopped to see any of it in my mind's eye. The Bible instructs us to write the vision down and make it plain[6], so distinctly that it can easily be carried out. In his book, *Think and Grow Rich*, Napoleon Hill[7] referred to it as the Definite Chief Aim. When we become serious about our dreams, they migrate from the space in our inventiveness to clear and concise steps toward manifestation. Visions motivate dreams. Dreams require goals.

Being the CEO of YOU involves integrating your dreams, visions, and goals into a personal development plan. Your visions should empower your dreams. Your dreams should aim to inspire and focus the journey to growth and self-discovery. Your goals should guide you to your fullest potential. On a given Sunday at The Experience Christian Ministries, while sitting in a charged and energetic church service, Pastor Shep shared a principle that will forever linger in my consciousness and effectively changed my pathway toward personal success and achievement. Among other success keys he shared, "The seed to completion is discipline." Furthermore, he taught, "The seed to the future is now." I understand that those are not new notions. Still, in that instance, just that quickly, I had my solution. The very next day, with intention, I created goals and deadlines for every endeavor I sought to accomplish. I knew far too well that without goals, dreams simply remain dreams never realizing success.

# 14

## Embrace Yourself

*"Become the person you needed when you were in need."*

-*Dr. Shalonda Crawford*

ou ARE greatness. Just as it is a fact that the sun is always shining, so too should the fact of your greatness endure. You are great even throughout all of your experiences no matter how good, hurtful, joyful, disappointing, and/or indifferent they may be. The fact of your greatness should allow you to be the sunshine that illuminates the spaces that you occupy. In spite of the occasional dark clouds and rainy days, the sun is always shining and so should you!

Embracing yourself authentically, is at the center of your personal growth and comprehensive overall well-being. We often place conditions on ourselves, *"If only I was able to* _____," or *"If only I had* _____," or *"I'd really be good at it if I* _____."

As for the blank spaces that you are able to fill in . . . get on with it. Fill them. Complete the task. And for those wishes and wantings that are outside of your control to change or implement . . . work toward acceptance. The more accepting of ourselves we are, the more attuned we are with our genuine inner selves, and the happier our lives are overall. Self-acceptance is our accomplishment of espousing all aspects of ourselves and not just the parts that we are proud to present.

To embrace you is to practice and master self-reflection and introspection and to gain a deeper understanding of who you are through your strengths, weaknesses, morals, and values. To do so with self-grace creates space for us to feel less stressed and more comfort when we are going through the difficult self-inspection process.

# 15

# The Healing Contingency

*"Place sunshine in the hearts of those who are hurting."*

-Dr. Shalonda Crawford

I t's never for nothing. All of our experiences have value, especially the hard, hurtful, and traumatic ones. The more hurtful they are, the greater the propensity and opportunity it presents you to utilize it as a healing agent. Experiences can cut like a knife, a sword in some instances. The deeper the cut, the more power the potential for a life-altering testimony. As we are overcome by our testimonies, our sharing is the key to our healing.

Proceed toward healing with the boldness of a conqueror. Don't deliberately avoid the tough feelings and emotions that swell up during the storms and tornadoes of life. Move toward them. Run into them. It is not too late to fall into the calamities that we have been hiding from, avoiding or standing just on the outlying perimeters of. Yes it hurts, but the truth of the matter is that none of our painful emotions will last at its initial intensity forever if we allow ourselves to engage and deeply feel them. Feeling is a way to show up for self. It is not until we really take in the feelings of sadness, disappointment, frustration, confusion, etc., that we truly exercise self-compassion. The healing contingency includes coming to terms with the losses that we suffer and uncomfortable emotions that we struggle to manage.

Further, our own healing is essentially wrapped up in our willingness and ability to heal someone else. Therefore, the only wasted experiences we will ever encounter over the span of our lives are the ones that we are unwilling or unable to share. What may prevent us from being *unable* to share? There are two main issues that keep us from exposing our truths: unhealed wounds and unforgiveness.

If unhealed wounds and unforgiveness are the main characters in your story, the next few chapters will highlight a few of the most damming culprits in your supporting cast that you may need to work on in your effort to heal the hidden hurts that seek to loom around in the background of your life.

# V

# Part V: Wounds

*"Don't let the pain of your past struggles obscure your future potential."*
*-Dr. Shalonda Crawford*

# 16

# Unhealed Wounds

*"Silence can be as deafening as screaming."*

-Dr. Shalonda Crawford

P sychological, mental, and emotional pain can leave you struggling and perhaps even believing that you are simply stuck, with a *'this is life' attitude.* It can also leave you feeling disconnected from the world around you, numb to your emotions, and even unable to trust people in general. You may be asking yourself, "How do I talk to anyone about this painful experience, when I can barely stand to think about it myself?"

I understand. I truly do. It took me nearly 2 decades to bring myself to share some of my own deep-seated secret wounds. It's not out of the ordinary to find it difficult to recover from past events that are painful. Intuitively we know that just because time has passed doesn't mean that we aren't still deeply affected by an experience. This is particularly true if it happened during our childhood years. If you are anything like me, there are instances in life that take quite a while to process before we understand that what happened is not normal life, but an actual traumatic experience to recover from. Again, there are some things that we cannot 'just get over.'

But what happens when we don't recognize our painful events as trauma that should be addressed? Subconscious psychological distress can set in, and, in some cases, it can linger for long periods of time. You may find yourself depressed, anxious, or worried but unable to pinpoint why. You may experience intrusive memories or uninvited flashbacks. You may be prone to physical ailments like unexplainable headaches, stomach aches, muscle soreness, fatigue, or other physical illnesses. Without proper attention, unhealed wounds can be the cause or foundation for underlying stress.

Most of us are managing some form unaddressed emotional, mental, spiritual, and/or psychological experiences that have caused a trauma wound. No, you are not alone in this. The great news is that it is never too late to jump onto the road of recovery. Let's take a look at a few things you may do to mitigate and cope with your painful or traumatic experiences. [89]

- *Prioritize self-care.* Make an intentional effort to eat and sleep well, get regular physical activity, and spend time in nature, specifically getting adequate exposure to sunlight. Be sure to engage in activities that bring you joy and replenish your state of being like, art, music, meditation, writing, and relaxation.
- *Be patient.* Contrary to self-care, it is easy to get caught in a trap of isolation and withdrawal. Isolation and withdrawal from people, enjoyable activities, and healthy habits can prolong your stress, make you feel stuck, and keep you from your healing process. Be gentle with yourself as you try to gradually ease back into your normal routine of things.
- *Limit your social media and news intake and engagement.* Nowadays,

world news is at our fingertips all day every day with ease and accessibility. Too much negative news and too many traumatic impressions can increase your stress and weigh heavy on your mood. In short, be mindful of what you watch and listen to. Significantly reduce the amount of news and/or pop culture you consume or temporarily cut it out altogether while you regain mental stability.

- *Put off all major life decisions that can wait.* Major decisions like career changes, drastic appearance changes, relocating, making major purchases (homes, cars, etc.) can be stressful in and of themselves but even harder when managing unhealed wounds. If and when possible, put them off until you feel more stable and better able to make sound decisions with a clear mind.

- *Seek and lean into the support of your village, family, friends, and trusted associates.* When you feel ready to discuss your thoughts and feelings, expressing them can be a big relief. You may also ask them to assist you with some of your daily tasks and obligations to help relieve some of your stress until you can regain normalcy. Support from loved ones, and/or a mental professional, can get you back on track and soon in your groove again.

# 17

# Unforgiveness

*"Don't become the person to brighten up the room because you left it."*
                                                    *-Dr. Shalonda Crawford*

Forgiveness is most definitely one of the biggest investments to employ and to have in your reserves. It has also proven to be one of the more difficult tools to acquire. As much as forgiveness is a major asset, unforgiveness is its equal liability. Before we can enjoy the benefits of forgiveness, we should review the drawbacks of unforgiveness.

Forgiveness means different things to different people. But in general, from my observations of a few hundred people in professional as well as personal settings, I believe I can safely speak for most and venture that it involves an intentional decision to let go of resentment and anger and move towards acceptance and restoration. The act that hurt or offended you might always be with you. But working on forgiveness can lessen that act's grip on and over you and it can cut the offender's puppet strings from you.

*The Stigma of Forgiveness*

There are 2 MAIN reasons why people struggle with the idea of forgiveness and remain hitched to unforgiveness. To address them, let's begin by talking about what forgiveness is NOT. Forgiveness is not,

· an emotion
· restoration
· giving a pass or letting them off the hook.

How do you know you've completed the forgiveness process? You'll know that you are completely through the process when you are sincerely happy for the successes of your offender. That space may seem like a lot to take in when you're at the start line, and quite frankly, you may be right. Many people never make it through to the finish line for every person who has hurt them; the smaller the issue, the easier the practice is. But the goal is more about working the process to remove the strings of trauma attachment from that person to you. As long as there is unforgiveness at play, you remain psychologically and spiritually tethered to your offender as well as very easily offended in those areas of sensitivity.

Further, when you are emotionally attached to your offender you surrender puppet strings to them. The decision not to forgive, in many ways, will result in you giving over power and control. Unforgiveness will eventually turn your offender into your puppet master.

For example, early on in my own forgiveness journey, I found myself triggered by the mere mention of an offender's name. To occupy space in the same room with that person brought all of the pain of the experience and those hurtful memories instantly to the very front of my mind. Essentially, I was unable to be in the company of that person nor could I tolerate the mere mention of that name. In those instances, I felt my own ability to control my thoughts, feelings and reactions in the moment rapidly diminish without mutual satisfaction. It was not a two-way street experience because unlike me, my offender was not at all impressed or bothered by me, my presence, or my wounded feelings in return. In fact, they had carried on with life, all while I was stuck and left behind holding a bag of emotional injury and trauma. That realization was yet another that propelled me into the motivation necessary to cut the strings of unforgiveness. It had become even more clear to me that at the end of the day, as long as I was dwelling on and not healing from that pain, I would remain stuck while my offender was off living what appeared to be an enjoyable life, free of me and my struggle. When it is all said and done, I've discovered that unforgiveness keeps us tied to the pain and to the offender, while forgiveness is a way of escape. The choice of the matter is entirely up to you.

*Forgive and Remember*

Forget? No! As a matter of fact, if at all possible, don't forget a single thing. Remember all of it, every bit of it. The goal is to learn from it. Never repeat it. Heal from it. Heal so thoroughly and absolutely that you can recall what happened without the emotional pain that is attached to the incident. But never forget it. The concept of "Forgive and Forget" is also more recently referred to as *toxic forgiveness*. Toxic forgiveness is a maladaptive way of coping. It is a mechanism used to avoid conflict and settle difficult or unresolved feelings and thoughts. It's a cover up. Forgive and forget is a way to trick yourself into pretending to be unbothered by the words, presence, or behaviors of others, when the reality is something different. The problem is that we are not play acting. In real life, we do not truly forget or even move on unless our feelings are heard, acknowledged, and allowed. Otherwise, we repress.

Though denial is the most common psychological defense of all, *repression* is the most powerful and persuasive psychological defense that we can employ. Repression is dangerous because it operates in a sneaky and stealthy manner. In fact, repression lives in the unconscious mind and won't even inform you that it is in motion. To have repression on your staff is to access the ability to remove distressing memories from the forefront of your mind, pushing all of those unwanted mental toils into the sub- or unconscious mind. Repression is a powerful defense for survival and a sense of normalcy but very rarely the healthiest. So, beware.

What lives in the back of your mind? Ever wondered why you have a difficult time getting or feeling a sense of closeness to others? Repression may just be the culprit at play. At the least, repression may slim down the ability to connect with others at a close and intimate level. Without conscious awareness, repression may assist your insensitivity to negative or unpleasant emotions and be the explanation for your low tolerance of people when they are seen to be emotionally struggling.

The concept of toxic forgiveness suggests that you forgive the offensive behavior and continue on without acknowledging the harmful injury that was caused or to dismiss the need to hold the offender accountable for their actions or for their rightful part in the ordeal. *Suppression* on the other hand, is a mature, more healthy coping mechanism that allows us to block painful experiences from awareness until there is a better time to respond. In short, repression is unconscious as opposed to suppression which is largely voluntary.

Again, forgive and forget... not a great idea. Experience is often one of our greatest teachers, particularly when it hurts. Painful experiences are very difficult to forget, so why not turn that pain into power? It is not always advisable to make an effort to keep hurtful experiences and memories at the *front* of your mind. When we lean in or lead with the trauma of our lives, we risk self-sabotage. However, we do want memories to remain accessible, if for nothing else, so that we do not become repeat offenders. There is a lot that can be learned from each of our painful experiences. After all, how will we recognize red flags if not for an experience to caution them?

Forgiveness, however, should be extended immediately. As mentioned before, forgiveness is difficult conceptually, but it is also as simple as settling on the decision to do so. Working through the process of reconciling your feelings and supporting the decision to undertake it is a process done at a self-pace. Recall, you know you have completed the process of forgiveness when a genuine regard can be made for the success of the person who caused the offense. Said another way, when your peace is not disturbed at the offender's success, you've made it. Keep in mind, that the journey to forgiveness is not always swift or fully accomplished. Unforgiveness, however, leaves you stuck. And sadly, it's usually a lonely place.

*Just Let It Go...*

Just let it go? How? Why? No! If it were a mere choice, wouldn't we all *"just let it go"*? For starters, if we could, we most certainly would, "JUST let it go." This idea is yet another form of toxic forgiveness. The fact that we are hanging on to such pain and negative emotions is evidence that it is not something that we can simply do. No one wants or willfully chooses to be in the bondage of constant pain. Forgiveness doesn't mean forgetting or excusing the harm that was done to you. Forgiveness is not reconciliation or restoration. It also does not necessarily mean making up, engaging, or further interacting with the person who caused you the harm. In fact, it may be best for you to never contact them again, let alone restore or reconcile with them.

Forgiveness is essentially about you and you alone, although it may by default benefit others as well. Forgiveness brings with it a kind of peace that allows you to focus on *yourself* and helps *you* go on with life. Removing the word, "just" from the phrase, because it is such an unreasonable ask, and focusing solely on letting go, leaves you accountable for your own journey and also releases you from the responsibility of "payback" for your offender, if you so choose to be relieved.

# 18

# A Place For Empathy

*"Everyone you know is struggling with something. Be kind."*

-Dr. Shalonda Crawford

There is a magical agent in the application of empathy. Empathy is a wonderful tool to utilize in instances where the act and process of forgiveness is tough or challenging. In short, empathy is joining with someone to embrace their experience as much as you can imagine having the experience yourself. Empathy is the cornerstone of genuine connectedness and the foundation for kindness. It is the key to understanding the feelings and sometimes the decisions and behaviors of others. Empathetic people are more likely to enjoy rich connections with others, which lead to stronger, deeper, and meaningful bonds.

Empathy is often confused or conflated with sympathy but different from sympathy. Sympathy is the act of being present and open to the experiences of others, while empathy takes it a step further. One step more, with empathy you are able to place yourself in that person's shoes.

We obviously feel different types of connections and emotions with different people in different and certain situations. Ultimately, the most powerful factor that is the effective ingredient of empathy is the simple acts of seeing and acknowledging, therefore validating a person in real time. That mere joining is powerful and restorative.

Sometimes a spot of empathy is all you need to get you unstuck. Empathy is a gift that we give to others while gifting ourselves at the same time. Empathy creates a pathway to others that *is* a two-way street. It is not solely about what you do and how you show up for someone else; it also involves you sharing yourself in exchange with that person. Remember, your healing is wrapped inside of your willingness with wisdom, to assist others.

Why with wisdom? Because trust is required in order to authentically share. Trusting someone with your most inner thoughts and experiences is critical in building healthy and empathetic relationships in concert with them. So, listen and connect, but also share. It is not an absolute must, but that interchange should be mutual and go both ways.

# 19

# Regret

*"Why look back when you can't go back?"*

*-Pastor Shep Crawford*

R ecovering from regret is challenging at the least. Regret is our mind's attempt to reconcile disappointment. Regret is painful. As I glance over my life and note salient disappointments, I also note what I have done to prevent repetition. A number of times I have found myself in a tug of war with myself for trusting and allowing yet another person too close and in too deep too quickly. In those instances, I regret placing my trust in people who ultimately let me down. Like many, I have depended on folks that didn't show up or come through for me in the ways that I thought they should or that they told me they would. Placing trust in them has at times caused me to regret mistakes and relationships, which then led to me managing disappointments internally within myself.

A battle with regret is an experience that we all have in common and can come in both small and large packages. From being placed on time-out for lying about sneaking a cookie from the countertop at age 4 to giving a lucrative business prospect "a piece of your mind," and therefore, not closing the game-changing deal at age 44. Regardless of your age, regret hurts. We only experience regret over a bad outcome when, at some point in time, we believe we could have prevented the unfavorable consequence.

Regret is a very real reaction to a disappointing event in your life, a choice that was made and that we know or believe cannot be changed. It may stem from something said that cannot be retracted or something done that cannot be undone. It's one of those feelings you can't seem to shake. It's a heavy and intrusive negative emotion that can last for minutes or days, one you may ruminate on for years, or, sadly, some folks may be unable to shake it off over their entire lifetimes. Both regret and disappointment are branches on the tree of grief. Slightly different from disappointment, regret is grief stuck in a loop, repeating and replaying itself.[10]

Regret is essentially that dreaded thing that you've done to yourself. Nonetheless, if our regrets and disappoints are handled in a nurturing environment and community as opposed to being alone in isolation, we can all become healthy and develop ego strength in the face and recovery from them.

Don't be afraid to do the work. Don't run from it, run into it. Healing awaits. Here is an opportunity to tap into our spiritual powers to let go of experiences that disappointed us so that we do not fall into the cycle of regret all over again. The overarching goal is to eventually, sooner than later, arrive at the place of acceptance and settle into equanimity with the reality of what happened in tandem with what was and now what is. I, myself, am getting better about it. I realize that I'm not ruminating so long in the "why" space and spending more effective time in the "what now" arena. I personally try to fall into Proverbs

3:5, "Leaning not unto my own understanding," but surrendering my burdens and confusion in God and finding peace and solace in Him as my centered starting point. Not all, but most of my regrets have been spiritually flatlined. Disappointments, on the other hand, have proven a little harder to manage. I am yet moving from regret and resentment into employing recovery and reconnection.

*Regret Unchecked*

What's more dangerous is regret that lingers without a pointed or proactive effort to resolve it. Regret unchecked will lead to some form of self-sabotage. Self-sabotaging is anything that we do to hinder or prevent our own forward progression toward success or recovery. Dealing with regret is especially difficult because it's hard to get even with yourself. When someone mistreats or mishandles us, we have a tendency to settle the score and get even. One bad hand deserves another, right? But revenge gets thorny when the culprit is you. How do you get revenge on you? What is your own big payback? You can't beat yourself up, cuss yourself out, or cut yourself off.

We have to find a way to settle in and live at peace with ourselves in spite of our own transgressions. Now come on, even the best of us have had a hard time with that! To make matters worse, regret comes along with a barrel of the other negative emotions connected to it including remorse, sorrow, and helplessness, guilt, shame, disappointment, and grief. I'm certain we can come up with more. It can increase our stress, have a negative impact on our physical health, and throw off the balance of our hormone and immune systems. So, regret is not only unpleasant, but also literally unhealthy. These things have actually been thoroughly and scientifically assessed and researched on a number of occasions. Harboring regret can really take a toll. Good news though! Regret and remorse can be detrimental, but, believe it or not, it can also have health-giving qualities.

*Benefits of Regret*

How befitting it is that we can benefit from our regrets. How are you benefiting from yours? There's always a silver lining, so instead of waddling, make your best effort to find it. Where is that ray of sunshine? Regret can be beneficial if we can figure out where we can or already have gained insight into the situation to establish what the red flags were, which leads to not making and repeating the same mistakes again. In short, we benefit because regret and remorse signal the need for corrective actions, and we learn from that how to make better decisions.

Regret is universal. It is another of life's mandatory experiences. We are imperfect, fallible beings, so making mistakes is inevitable. At various points in our lifetimes, we will have many regretful experiences, most of us will have plenty. That can actually be good news depending on how we employ it and to which role you assign it.

As far as that thing, whatever that thing is for you, the issue of regret that is right now, at the forefront of your mind, it too can also find a meaningful place. Allow yourself a swig of relief. Without mistakes we are simply not living. The proof is in the numbers. Not just a few of us but all of us have made or are currently making mistakes. Mistakes allow us an opportunity to learn, grow, stretch, and ultimately change. We have none of that without a misstep.

Even though regret may birth positive change, it is more commonly associated with the negative effects that it can have on our overall happiness and well-being. It's worth it to get to the bottom of the matter and make every attempt to resolve it once and for all. We know what happened and what we did to contribute to it. Now it's time to identify the "why" of your regret. Discover why it is so profound and properly label it as such. Often the route to why reveals more about our personal values and feelings, create greater self-awareness, self-understanding, and ultimately more compassion, meaning, and purpose.

In short, here are 5 quick tips that we can employ to begin the process of recovering from regret:

1. Acknowledge mistakes or poor decisions.
2. Give yourself the grace you want from others.
3. Pull out the lesson.
4. Make amends with others, if needed.
5. Let it go, live on, and do better.

Exhale. You are on the road to recovery.

# 20

## Overdoing What Was Underdone

*"Feeling left out makes you question your worth, but remember, you're enough with or without their validation."*

-Unknown

Empty. After several instances of performing before "standing room only" crowds, it finally dawned on me that the rooms were ceaselessly void of a cheering squad that was specifically designated for me. For me. Not the team. Not the school. Not the general sport. Not my friend's parents, but a little *"whoot-whoot!"* just for me. My support corner seemed to exist by the default crowd of regular attenders. Time after time. Game after game. Performance after performance. Eventually, I became empty and numb of it. Disappointment is precipitated by expectation. Where there is no expectation, there is also no disappointment. By the time I made it to college, I had zero expectations and absolutely zero feelings left. Who cares? Over time, I stopped looking for support. I never stopped wanting it, but I stopped expecting it. I stopped being disappointed. Or did I?

To be fair, my parents were teenagers when they had me, their firstborn. Looking back now as an adult, my parents were in their early

30s when I was in middle school and only in their mid 30s when I was in high school. It's much easier to recognize now that they were also understandably trying to live young life. They were imperfect young adult people raising me, an imperfect person. Still, my reality was then and is now what it is nevertheless.

Have you ever pondered, "*Why does this bother me so much?*" Though I'd made up in my mind that I would no longer be burdened by the lack of what I perceived as support in some areas of my life, the subconscious burden still remained tucked away in the back of my mind. The feeling, the questioning, and wondering about my worthiness, unbeknownst to me, actually had been resting just beneath the surface. I had not yet grasped the language to identify and label this state of being, but I was aware of the yearning and restlessness that I battled. Void. There, underneath the meh and nonchalant, was a quiet inner call. A quiet call. The kind of quiet, that when not careful, never failed to blare out in my decisions and then actions. The lack of support, whether real or perceived, has created a void in me that is still alive today. It influences my choices, flavors my worldview, and impacts my priorities, but it also incites passion in my heart.

What is it to live with a void? The void is the gap between who we are, what we feel at the core, and the ego that we have learned to replace it with. It is the distance between the authentic self and the self-image that we try to disguise it with. Hiding the true self is a learned behavior. Voids employ the masks that the true self hides behind. After so many disappointments, I stopped expecting anyone to show up and rather than deal with the hurt that it caused, I found a hiding place. I hid behind the '*I don't care*' mask. Hiding hurts too but it's safer there. I knew what to expect.

We all deal with different forms of voids, and we are all in various stages of bridging the gaps of their existence. We are all flawed beings. Our imperfect experiences and then our perceptions of them have caused us to become mentally and emotionally fragmented. It's a patient rub. To varying degrees, we are all wearing fragmented masks that, over time, progressively rub away at the reality of our wholeness. Do you know what you are covering up? Are you aware of your mask? Most of us are not aware of our voids and are arbitrarily getting along with life in spite of it. Except we are not. Somewhere in our lives the void that has caused us to have gaping emotional and mental holes is insatiably demanding to be refilled. Over the years, I have employed a few different disguises that I tend to rely on to fill mine that depend on the pain at hand. Drinking, sexing, over and underdressing, lying, smiling, mean-mugging, makeup, over and undereating, intellectual conversation, flossing, judging, and bragging are all masks that I have employed in my attempts to fill the voids in my life. All of them so satisfying in the moment, but also short-lived with stale endings. Without an understanding of my own issues, I could never fill the emptiness that feels like a deep, dark, blunted, bottomless hole.

When we discover that vices do not work, grasping at straws, we may be tempted to lean into deeds and actions. The problem is that when we are operating out of our unquenchable voids, we deceivingly exert our efforts in overdoing what was underdone for us. Because I believed that I did not have a cheering squad of die-hard supporters rooting me on in the activities and engagements that I deemed important, I made a point to be just that for my children. I mean I made sacrifices and missed out on personal and professional opportunities to be at their events that were, on more than a few occasions, unreasonable and even unwise to miss. I was in the audience, on the bleachers, and in the room at times when they'd assured me that I really didn't need to be.

On a few occasions, I noticed them flavor their pleads with a pleasant, "*No really mom, we're good.*" But no, not Supermom Me! How could I miss an event? Big or small, I had to let them know, "*No it's totally okay. I really want to be there for you.*" For them? Yeah . . . no. I have since realized that I was showing up for them in the way that I had longed for my parents to show up for me. Trauma is a trip. I wanted a parent's attendance so badly at certain events that I'm certain my memory is skewed. Thinking back now, I honestly couldn't tell you how many people were in my cheering corner. I just know that it didn't matter because the people I longed for were not. So, what did I do for my children? Yup, you guessed it. I put on the mask of Supermom and showed up at all of their events to save *myself* from disappointment.

What are you overdoing? Are you a people-pleaser or an over-accommodating "yes" person because you were under-attended to? Are you a feisty, no-nonsense, straight-shooter, who lets everyone know exactly what is on your mind because you were silenced at a time when your emotions were screaming out? Were you not allowed to speak when you had something so very important to say? Was your input or opinion dismissed? Are you the larger than life beat of the party or the class clown because you're really hiding behind the tears caused by the relentless ridicule that you endured? The void-behavior is usually invited to the party but ultimately an unwelcomed guest.

What was underdone? Do you long for attention, validation, nurture, acceptance, discipline, reassurance, approval, confidence, or peace? As for me, I was no better than any other average parent, including my own for that matter. Who knew? From my own subjective view, I was simply overdoing what was underdone for me.

# 21

# Don't Avoid the Voids

*"Emotional sickness is avoiding reality at any cost. Emotional health is facing reality at any cost."*

-M. Scott Peck

What is the nature of your void? Is it emotional, mental, spiritual, financial, or relational? Identify it. Not knowing what your nemesis is can be as exhausting as battling the wind. We will never defeat or hit a target that we cannot identify. Let's not forget to recall why it showed up in the first place. Did your void overhear a conversation with your best friend and another friend that left you feeling insignificant? Maybe it was the promotion that your co-worker got on the job that filled you with jealousy and envy. Or was it the judgment that you assessed of yourself as you passed by the hallway mirror? Until we resolve this unaddressed trauma, we are essentially living someone else's life, while simultaneously in search to find our true selves with unconditional acceptance.

What happened to the vulnerability that we once had as a kid? What is inherently wrong with being gullible? There is a level of trust that is required to be vulnerable or gullible. Life has taught us to tuck them away. Wouldn't life be grand if we could "just be" who we really are? We all have two very innate desires: to be loved and to be accepted. But there is a very important caveat. We want to be loved and accepted for who we authentically and genuinely are, without the masks that we have learned to solicit.

Life teaches us the importance of self-restraint. Discipline is good. It keeps us regulated and controlled. Voids reinforce the impulse to apply the brakes on the happy-go-lucky and carefree outlook that we once had. The consequence is that we ultimately become deceived of our own plans. Eventually, we think we *are* the masks. We forget that we were putting them on just to get past the moment, to get through the experience, to deal provisionally. Some of us have made the mask a permanent fixture. Now the mask stands between the spontaneity and vulnerability of being our genuine selves and upholding the image that we have safely been projecting.

The voids that our life experiences caused us were not life dealing you a bad hand. They have a wealth of value if we learn how to envision, appoint, equip, and manage them. Voids are not meant to rain on our pursuits of happiness but rather the opposite. Mostly, voids are ineffective communicators trying to send a message. Let's try for a moment to stop working to satiate our voids and just listen to them. Time spent exploring and becoming intimately familiar with our void areas is an investment well spent. Embracing them, understanding them, and gleaning from them can extract a richer experience of personal depth, increase, and growth.

# 22

# Desert Seasons

*"Do everything you can and then relax. It's now out of your hands, but God is in control."*

-Dr. Shalonda Crawford

The desert is vast and wide, hot, and dry. It is not a popular tourist spot. With intention, people avoid desert destinations. It is a lonely place. Loneliness is painful. At some point on the life journey, we will all make a pit stop in the desert. The desert is the place and an opportunity for you to be introduced to you. Many people find it difficult to be alone. Primarily because of past trauma, having prolong periods of time with only self can even be excruciating for some.

There are those who prefer to be alone. There are those who delight in a healthy amount of isolation. For them, the ability to withdraw from the world and retreat into places of solidarity is a welcomed and even favored occasion. But if you are anything like me, to the contrary, isolation, quiet time, lights off, and seclusion can be like a punitive quarantine. Those of us who are used to the comfort of companionship may struggle to be alone if not also used to having prolonged undisturbed time designated to self.

In either case, it is a challenge for most of us to bear the discomfort of alone time in a desert season when there are issues of experiential pain, fear, abandonment, and trauma to contend with. For those who retreat to avoid facing or to mask issues, the desert process of being alone may exacerbate any symptoms and experiences that have been distracted from and consequently expose any existing, stuffed mental health conditions. Research suggests that periods of involuntary isolation and loneliness can cause and/or increase stress. Anxiety, depression, sleep challenges, and low motivation and esteem are likely and anticipated desert guests.

On the other end, let us not forsake or forget the value of the desert. Remember, this is the time for you to get a deeper sense and understanding of who you are at your own core and essence. It is a time for evaluation to deeply reflect and inventory your circles of social, professional, spiritual, friends, family, and community. A desert season extends an opportunity to introspectively delve into divine and life purpose. It is the "get to know me better" order of the day. How are you able to improve and enhance your natural gifts, interests, hobbies, experiences, personality, and spiritual relationship? Achieving a deeper understanding of yourself causes you to live life proactively on the offense verses reactively on the defense. If you embrace and utilize your time wisely in the desert, you exit a wiser decision-maker with a better ability to choose and assess your interactions and responses to people and opportunities more carefully. Alternatively, you avoid subconscious sabotage and previous maladaptive wallowing in challenges, situations, and sensitive emotions.

Take on the full advantage of your desert season. Be curious about yourself. Explore your interests. Explore the things that God has in store for you. Designate committed time for prayer and meditation to listen and hear from Him. Be receptive and aware of the colorful differences that color your canvas among different people and accept that your differences are what make you wonderfully made and uniquely individual. You are a crafted masterpiece.[11] You are not everyone's cup of tea and not everyone is yours. Accept that you are not assigned to everyone and not everyone is assigned to you. That remains Jesus's job. Self-awareness builds and fosters better ways to produce and cultivate healthy and enjoyable relationships in the fullness of time.

# 23

# Problems and Answers

*"Your story is a blueprint that can guide someone else's journey."*

*-Dr. Shalonda Crawford*

Whose problem do you assist? Whose prayers are you the answer to? As you contemplate your route out of the desert, it may be helpful to consider aligning yourself with your life's purpose. Life purpose is more about who you are called to than it is about you. Who are you called to? Who leans into your light? Who can see and identify your glow? Who appreciates your warm and luminous radiation?

Our fulfillment, gratitude, and sense of overall life accomplishment will be found in our efforts for others. Furthermore, those that we are called to will appreciate us, see us, acknowledge us, and welcome our contributory gifts and talents. Those called to us do not take us for granted. Remember, our life's experiences, exposure, skills, talents, and worldview are uniquely designed to position us to be a solution.

There are a few key steps we can take to discover whose problem we are the answer and solution to.

*Strength.* First, spend time in introspection connecting with the areas of yourself that you naturally excel in. What are the gifts and talents that come to you naturally? What are your strengths and skills? Your natural abilities are the tools to assist you with the problems that you are suited to solve.

*Passion.* Next, discover and note the core principles that are important to you. Give deep thought and reflect on the issues, the causes, and the dilemmas that resonate with you beyond the surface level. We all have a natural and innate passion for humankind but take some time to go beyond that. Topics, issues, and people that you are more drawn to and spark your enthusiasm for change can guide you toward a commitment to actively be a part of those resolves.

*Evaluate.* Further, take an assessment of the needs and challenges of the people who are in your proximity. What is the composition of your community networks and circles in relation to society at large? Consider how your unique and individual proficiencies and passion can provide a positive imprint and impact in addressing those needs.

*Action.* Even a single step in the right direction can make a big splash in the life of a person in need. Let us not forsake the benefits of small steps in the right direction toward addressing the problems that bring your purpose into line.

*Reflect.* Spend regular and intentional time in reflection about your experiences, observations, interactions, and the impact that you are making. Deepen your imprint. Make your mark as you make a difference in the life or lives of others. Reflection in combination with self-awareness and action will reveal whose problems you are uniquely equipped to solve, whose prayers you are called to answer and the clarity you need for your own life's purpose.

# 24

# The Gift of Failure

*"One may fail copiously, but no one is crafted a failure."*

-Dr. Shalonda Crawford

istakes only remain mistakes if we choose not to search and seek the lesson in every failed attempt. We have a great choice. Stay in the classroom of life or sit fearfully on the sidelines with regret. It may sound a bit counterintuitive . . . the *gift* of *failure*. How is or can failure be a gift? Let us delve very briefly into how to we can unwrap and open our gifts of failure. If you are anything like the average person, your gifts have been left under the Christmas tree for several years now. Normalizing the fact that in some form, shape, fashion, or another, we've all endured failure, is not only reassuring but also a cause for relief. Most of us have had at least one experience that could be described as an epic failure. If by some slight chance you're one of the few that have not, just keep right on living! I am firsthand knowledgeable.

After a quick reflection and review, I have listed a few of my failures so far and I suggest you make a list as well.

- I failed the California state licensure exam for psychologists.
- I failed the California real estate exam.
- I failed my written driver's test the first two times I took it.
- I failed to the Pom-Pom squad audition in middle school and the cheerleading team during my freshman year in high school.
- On many occasions, I failed to get call-backs from jobs, plays, music and commercial auditions.
- I've failed at landing the 'perfect' job too many times to count.
- I have failed in romantic and intimate relationships.
- I have been completely lost in areas of confidence and self-esteem and lost in terms of lived life.
- I've failed at making myself a priority. Because of that, I've learned that if I'm on the back burner, the things in my life marinate but are never well-done.
- I've failed at friendship.
- I've failed at showing gratitude, respect, and appreciation.
- I've failed at being my authentic self.

And then . . . I recovered.

Like everyone else, I am a work in progress that is on a ceaseless pendulum of falling, failing, recovery, restoration—repeat. But because of those cycles and series of failures, I love much deeper. If you're a friend of mine, I appreciate you much more openly. I now have a strong and rich opinion of the importance of relationships in general— all because I've failed in that area. Exposure is what brings us into knowing. We do not know what we know until we are exposed to it. Here is an interesting tidbit that I fully agree with from Greg Ward[12], "*Many successful people have said that their biggest failures became their greatest inspirations. It is something that drives them to succeed next time."*

Though failure is inevitable, here is the good news to hang your hat on and keep your spirit intact long enough to endure the failure process. There is no success without failure because there is nothing to learn from without mistakes—FAILURE! Every successful person and every successful story will include missteps, mistakes, and what many may consider flat-faced disappointment.

Don't believe me? Do your own research. Google the back story of any person that you consider or respect as successful, and, if they are honest, you will find the areas and experiences that they have failed in. I have learned through many of my own hurts, disappointments, and missed opportunities, as well as critical self-assessments that it was all a set up. Those very experiences—sometimes the ones that I was too ashamed to share, were the training ground and the boot camp that was necessary to prepare me for a larger platform.

Through a recent series of "failures," I realized there are vast opportunities to change the attitudes of others and to inspire hope in some folks that may be on the brink of giving up on a dream or a hope or even a notion. But if only I could and would be bold enough to first acknowledge and then admit my own weaknesses and struggles, they may be helped. I've concluded that our dreams—meaning whatever we aspire to do or whomever we aspire to become, must include the exposure of our ENTIRE journey so far and to highlight those bumps in the road. Bumps in the road actually assist the dream once we finally arrive at it.

Learning that failure is merely a part of the process is a powerful tool for dream building. Highlighting the benefits of negative experiences can provide a fresh new perspective on our forward-moving process as well as learning how to turn the disadvantages of failure into life and character advantages. Exploring ways to strategize and discover how to allow those painful experiences to inspire us, to push us, to grow us, and NOT to break us is a bonus schema. That shortcoming, the one that keeps coming to mind, the one that is presently on your mind right now, has the potential to produce the real progress needed for your own reform. It should, if directed properly, motivate you to action. Let us embrace and take action.

*Here are 6 ways That Failure Can Be a Gift to You*

### Failure Builds Compassion

Failure, oftentimes, fits neatly in the box with grief and loss. Failed efforts can take a toll. Have you ever found yourself comforting a person who has been through a painful ordeal? It is really hard to laugh at the person who lost the race, or didn't make it to the finals, or was beaten in the match. From the outside and in the stands it's all fun and games. But if that loser is your close friend or family, you're pouring out all the compassion you can muster up to help them get through it. Why? Well, obviously you don't want to see your loved one hurt but also because on some or on many levels, you can relate. In those moments when you're called upon to comfort a friend, your ability to genuinely tap into that joining power is the compassion you have because you have been in an unfortunate position in some way at some point yourself.

### Failure Fortifies and Builds Character

The mere act of us facing head-on the mental burden that comes on us when we fail, in and of itself, is another way to build character. The more failed experiences we have, the more we develop the ability to bounce back, enrich our faith, and cultivate a deeper understanding of who we are at our core. We are resilient! We just have to tap into the resilience. It is there.

You've fallen short. Okay. Remember you're in good company. Now, get yourself up, dust yourself off, and try again, and again, and again and however many agains it takes to get to the other side. That's one way we can increase our mental fortitude, be on guard, and be prepared for failure that *will* come up later. Managing to pick ourselves up and start again can prove that we are working that heart and that mental muscle that builds up strength of character.

Failure helps us get to realistically KNOW the parts of us that we may want to improve or move on from. We are not meant to do everything. When we figure out what we are and are not good at, we will find ourselves embracing our weaknesses without judgment and honing our strengths with greater self-deference. Strength of character is also shown in our abilities to respect the things that we can do but also cannot do or are not very good at doing.

*Failure Sharpens Critical Thinking*

Critical thinking is one of the most valuable assets to have in life. It is the knack of being able to objectively analyze and evaluate and review whatever our issues or situations are and then make informed judgments about them. With the right perspective and mindset, the more times we fail, the more we begin to bounce back *faster* because we develop the ability to find new approaches to new solutions faster. Critical thinking, even meta thinking, which is to think about the way you think, are assets that we can sharpen in response to failure.

When we are meta thinking—thinking about *why* it happened, then by default, we are also critically gaining a deeper perspective and understanding of where to assign blame, or whether there is a *blame* in play at all. Here is a great place to speak to those who have really struggled inside of failure. Oftentimes and most commonly, when we do not meet the mark, we begin to look inward to personal deficiencies like not being capable, or not being good enough, or even that we don't deserve whatever the goal was. The thinking in these cases is as if we are to blame rather than critically assess the circumstance or even the timing and other factors that may be involved in the process. Moreover, bouncing back over time creates inner strength and toughness if we allow it. With the right perspective and mindset, we build up the motivation and determination not to fail again and we are better able to avoid the same mistakes when we are critical thinkers. Hence, we memorialize the imposter syndrome.

### Failure Is Your Greatest Asset

Almost every new initiative that we take on is trial and error. Life can essentially be seen as a hands-on experiment. It is critical that we leave a space for things *not* to go right or as planned. Successful people run analysis reports on their experiences in life. Without the analysis report, we just continue in a cycle of the same ol' disappointments. It is literal insanity. Expecting different results by doing the same ol' thing is a hard stop, "no"!

Failed attempts provide confirmation that a thing is not the best or that it actually is our vehicle to improved, bigger, and better outcomes. If we sacrifice time spent in introspection and reflection to assess what worked, what did not work, and why, the payoff will be a better end game. Do not miss the opportunity to make your failed attempts a proven asset to your updated plan. Spend time figuring out what you can do and how you *can* think differently.

### Fear of Failure is Even Worse than Failure Itself

Be clear. It is absolutely normal to be fearful of failure. It is also difficult for most of us to accept not being "good enough." But what is good enough? What is the measuring stick that defines or determines what is acceptable, satisfactory, or good enough for you. In some cases, it is laid out for us; you need 70% on the test, or it must be done within 5 minutes, completed and submitted by August 11th, etc. Have you even taken a moment to ponder for yourself what good enough is? For example:

There is a 200–800 score range for the California state licensure exam for a psychologist. The minimum passing score is 500. Hear me clearly when I tell you that after 5 failures on this particular exam, I was not trying to be a rockstar. Good enough in this case *for me* was 500. Period. End of story. Issue me my California state license. Thank you very much!

Nevertheless, I believe that a large part of my failing was about the amount of fear I took into the testing center with me about not passing. In many ways we set ourselves up for failure by our own internal beliefs about what we can and cannot accomplish. I wholeheartedly believe that considering and then accepting the possibility that I would not pass the test, was largely the reason why on so many occasions, I didn't.

Again, like a leaf of pain, failure is a part of the life experience. There is no way around it. We cannot be successful in everything that we do. No amount of money can be paid to avoid it. Moreover, if you are exerting excessive amounts of energy and spending considerable amounts of time trying to live a completely cautious life for fear of failure—NEWS FLASH—you are officially not living at all. By default, you are moving in opposition of your fullest potential.

*Failing Forward*

Mistakes only remain mistakes if we don't learn from them. If we do this thing right, we'll always fail FORWARD. What have you learned from your past mistakes? Here are two questions to ponder: What is your greatest failure and what did you learn from it? There is often a lot more substance in the answer to that question than that of success. Failing backwards is when you blame other people, situations, and misfortunes for your mistakes. No accountability. Though we may in fact be an occasional victim of circumstances, we should also on occasion be able to see where we played a part in our own shortcomings and/or where we could have or should have done something differently. Failing backwards is when we neglect to take inventory or reflect and then keep making the same mistakes repeatedly while genuinely believing that things will change or be different. Again, we fail backwards when we lack tenacity and endurance, when we turn inward and see ourselves as a failure as opposed to a person that failed at something. This maladaptive schema leaves us vulnerable to taking things personally and ultimately forming the self-sabotaging habit of quitting. That's backwards. Others are overcome with anxiety and choose to completely tap out. Laying down in indecision leaves us jammed up and in the danger of being stuck in the painful middle.

We unlock the gift of failure when we learn to accept it as the essential steppingstone that leads to the garden of success. If we truly want to reach our best potential, navigate life more confidently, meet our dreams, and achieve our goals, we will embrace the idea that the greatest and best lessons are learned when we fall short. That is how we fail forward.

One of the biggest obstacles that keep folks from success is the fear of failure. Failure can paralyze us and keep us safe but can also keep us from ever achieving the greatest version of self. No risk taken, no opportunity for elevation. Simple. Point blank. Try it. If it doesn't work? Reflect, analyze, and try again. Repeat the process a few times, taking notes each time. Then you can decide. What have you learned? How have you or can you grow from it? Has the failure taught you to continue forward or pursue in a different direction? And then finally, pay it forward. How can you use it to help someone else?

In summation, we will fail again. Those with the greatest success understand that failure is simply one of the many steppingstones to success and an intricate part of the process. Never let failure stop you from chasing your dreams. Furthermore, the next time you fail, unwrap your gift. Cash in on your lessons and change your life's perspective.

# 25

# Doing vs. Being

*"There is always a me behind me that's got my back. "*
                                            *-Dr. Shalonda Crawford*

I can fail a test, but I am not a failure. I failed that dang on test 5 times and still, I am not a failure. There are so many things that we can do but nothing can impede on who we are at our core. Let us pause here to quickly highlight a huge misconception. There can be a vast difference between the inner you and your actions, your behaviors, and the things that you are seen doing. Though doing and being often walk and work hand and hand, they are not conjoined and can therefore operate apart or in tandem. As the CEO of YOU, the choice is yours.

Our being is synonymous with our essence. Being is who we are at the center. Being involves our sense of self, as it relates to our belief and value systems. Our being mirrors our reflections of self and encourages or discourages self-awareness and acceptance. Being is at the seat of inner contentment or displaced at discontentedness. On the other hand, doing is just that. It supposes the actions that we take, the behaviors we employ, and the choices we actually make. It can entail positive practices like goal setting and achievements. But doing can also be to our own detriment and self-sabotage like in the form of procrastination and perfectionism.

Realizing the contrast between being and doing in my own work in therapy with my therapist, proved to be the illumination that I needed to muster the necessary morale and courage to take the licensure test for the fourth, fifth, and finally the sixth times. For me it was discovering the sense of balance between the two realities that co-mingled inside of me. Or better yet, mustering the strength of self and authentic identity, to completely merge them.

On many occasions, I definitely struggled to distinguish and separate my actions from my essence. When I lost my virginity at 15 and then ended up pregnant, I was immediately labeled by many as a fast-ass little teenage girl. How sad. Now, as true as it is that my doing led to pregnancy, I was by no means a "fast-ass." In the reverse, for a while my title became, "sad teen mom." Even then, before I fully understood the difference, I understood the need for distinction. I was determined to separate labels like sad, poor-girl, and naïve from my own self-impressions and rather continue pressing toward the confidence and grit at the core of me.

Misconceptions about what we do verses who we are is a huge obstacle in the way of confidence and thus success. If we become too focused on what we have done, albeit forced or voluntarily, we chance our overall well-being and often at the peril of inner fulfillment. Nevertheless, getting overly centered on being, at the expense of constructive action, can lead to paralysis, arrest, and stagnation of goals and the pursuit of happiness in life. When we turn inward and see ourselves as a failure as opposed to a person that failed at something—the fundamental mistake we are making is that we begin to conflate who we are as an individual with what we have done. That is dangerous on both sides of the coin of failure *and* success. What we do does not define who we are but rather expresses where we are captured in that moment. I had a child at a young age, but I am not sad or in need of pity. I failed a test but I'm not a failure. And neither the end of my story.

# VI

# Part VI: Pitfalls

*"Good things do not come easy. The road is lined with pitfalls."*
*–Desi Arnaz*

### PITFALLS THAT PREVENT EMPLOYMENT

*What are pitfalls? Pitfalls are those sly and unforeseen life events that quarterback sneak us in an attempt to ruin our life's plan. We've all been ditched or faced a major roadblock or two that hindered us from our progress. The good news is that we have more control over those cunning pitfalls than we may have ever imagined. Here are a few...*

# 26

# Terminal Uniqueness

*"Being me brings joy to me."*

*-Dr. Shalonda Crawford*

Terminal *Uniqueness* is the idea that an experience is so vastly special or different from anyone else's that the person alone has uniquely experienced or is experiencing it. Terminal uniqueness is also referred to as *personal exceptionalism* and is commonly a struggle for people trying to find stability from forms of addiction. A person dealing with this issue believes that they are the exception to the norm and that their circumstance(s) is completely different from anything else that others have experienced. People who battle with the schema of terminal uniqueness believe that they are the only ones in the world that feel the way they do, that only they struggle the way they do, and, as a result, only they think the way that they do. It is hard for them to fathom that plenty of people share in their struggles to some degree, form, or fashion because they have never encountered anyone like them in a shared experience. Further to the contrary, their experience has been encounters of shame, ridicule, guilt, and rejection as opposed to any sense of understanding. Though the unicorn feeling is real, it is absolutely the furthest from the truth.

The reason why terminal uniqueness is the first pitfall on the list is because it is by far one of the most dangerous. Healing happens in community, and despair is confirmed in isolation. When people believe that they are terminally unique, their thinking, by default, insinuates that no one else has ever recovered from or conquered it. Because they are alone in the experience and unaware of anyone else ever having been in such a situation, they tend to hang on to the idea that they are unique. The belief is then doubled by the thought that no one else can help, no one else can relate or offer valid advice to realistically assist them, and, most devastating, no one else can guide them to true healing and peace because there is no one with direction that really knows the way.

Based on those that I have encountered who struggle with this mindset, there are 2 major schemas at play: (1) a lack of intrinsic self-value and (2) an inability to justify or explain *being* different (because subjectively they *feel* different) from and outcast from everyone else over the course of their lifetime. The confusion is inoculating because though they are just as human as anyone else, they are unable to genuinely connect to anyone else.

The state of confusion or unknowingness can cause clinginess. Ultimately, they tend to hang on tightly to the pain. The pain is familiar. The pain is predictable. The pain is dependable. And as much as there is a desire to separate from it, people suffering from terminal uniqueness hold on to their pain as if their lives depend on it. Furthermore, they truly believe that it does.

Conceptually understanding terminal uniqueness may be simple but consciously recognizing the signs of it for you or someone you know may be illusive. We all want to be unique and/or exceptional which makes it all the more difficult to determine when this maladaptive worldview is at play. Here are a few signs to look out for:

- Feeling like no one can relate to you
- Frequently comparing yourself to others (the comparative measuring stick)
- An insatiable need for attention
- Putting others down or one-upping them
- An inability to relate or hold space for the ideas, opinions, or approaches that are different from your own

If you believe that you or someone you know who may be dealing with terminal uniqueness, here are a few tips to address it:

- Employ an open mind
- Look out for similarities and common ground as opposed to looking for differences
- Lean into what you know as opposed to how you feel
- Make an effort to forge genuine connections with other people
- Lastly, seek the professional assistance of a mental health professional as needed

# 27

# Accept Not Being Accepted

*"Acceptance is embracing what actually is and then making the proper adjustments."*

-Dr. Shalonda Crawford

Rejection.

That is what not being accepted feels like. But why though? Because not everyone is your "folks." Not every community or gathering of people are your village. Not all blood-related kin are your family. We all experience feelings of rejection in situations or interactions that do not embrace us. If we can begin by acknowledging that feelings of rejection or lack of acceptance are a natural response and part of the human experience, then we can normalize the experience when those feelings come up.

*Inward Exploration*

Pulling yourself up from your bootstraps is never an easy accomplishment, primarily because we are naturally drawn to be and do things within community and with the assistance, encouragement, and validation of those around us. Finding ourselves void of affirmation is an indication that an inward shift needs to occur. We should explore our own values, strengths, beliefs, and moral compasses aside our families or generational norms. It is a tough mountain to climb but by doing so we build up and cultivate a stronger sense of self-awareness which naturally equates to self-worth that is not reliant on outsider interference or external validation. Inner exploration allows us the freedom to discover uniqueness and to embrace unadulterated individuality. Cut out and reframe the negative self-talk as well as any capped thoughts linked to not being accepted by others.

*Nah. I'm Good*

Feeling on the outskirts never feels good, but boundaries are all the more important from the sidelines. Do not allow your pain to cause you to neglect honoring yourself and your needs, values, respect, and overall well-being.

*Bask in Your Sunshine*

Seek out and be intentional about nurturing the relationships that actually do accept and appreciate you for who you are authentically. Be mindful to surround yourself with them in an effort to experience and reestablish a sense of support, understanding, and true connection that is rooted in a genuine and mutual exchange. Be encouraged to accept not being accepted by recalling your resilience, be self-assured because of your overcoming, and be reminded of your self-empowerment and inner strength as evidenced by your accomplishments. Find first, the validation and acceptance from within, which ultimately will inspire others and lead to a more authentic and fulfilled life, with and without the acceptance of anyone else.

# 28

# The Comparative Measuring Stick

*"Comparison with myself brings improvement, comparison with others brings discontent."*

— Betty Jamie Chung

B eware of the comparative measuring stick.

There is a fundamental danger in employing the comparative measuring stick as the means to determine your personal status, value, and/or requirements for yourself. Too much comparison leads to a watered-down self-image, self-esteem, unhappiness, frustration and feeling "not good enough." How many presentations by motivational speakers have you watched and listened to online and thought, *I could never captivate an audience like that.* And here's one that most of us are guilty of. How many times have you crossed a person in passing and said to yourself, *I wish I was as wealthy or as successful as them.* How many times have we done it? You see a celebrity or influencer posting on social media about their relationship and think to yourself, *I want a Boo like that, or I wish I had a fly sense of fashion and style.* Don't fall for it. It's a trap.

Insert here the illusion of social media. I have said it often. People post on social media for the world to see, the impressions or parts of them they want seen. For the most part, we are privy to any given person's public persona. And, if we are not careful—what we will do is find ourselves believing the projected perceptions cast out from people who are hiding what's really happening or going on privately with them. Imagine that. Listen, guard against the comparative measuring stick. By any means necessary, avoid it. And whatever you do, don't be caught up in the illusive web of comparing yourself to someone else's mirrored or imagined ideal for themselves.

There is nothing wrong with utilizing the accomplishments of your mentors, role models, and people of high inspiration as markers to aspire to. Nothing wrong with keeping good company, wise counsel, and striving for better. It's actually the recommended practice. However, if you are unable to hang on to your own identity and personal vision for yourself with and apart from them, you are then more likely to begin developing feelings of diminished self-worth.

Comparing yourself to another essentially disregards the road you've traveled to get where you are. It negates all of the blood, sweat, and tears that you have endured to get here. In comparison, disregarding your reality is literally fantasizing the past differently from what it actually was.

Insecurity is perpetuated by its comparison of security. Insecurity is universal. It's normal to measure yourself up against others. Even the most confident people do it at times. The difference is that confident people may visit a comparison or two every now and then, but they do not live there. Remember, you are the sum total of *your* experiences. Your past is exclusive. It's your greatest schoolteacher. The past produced today's badge of honor. Use your past as the yardstick of comparison. It alone has shaped and molded you. It cannot and should not be compared as an evaluative measure with anyone else. The only real competition that you have is with who you were yesterday, last year, a decade ago. That leaves you in competition with you. Look back through the rearview mirror of your life with retrospection. Of course, you have more growing to do, but you've come so far. Aren't you proud of you? Reflect.

Again, who you are presently, on the other hand, can be influenced and inspired by others that you admire and look up to but never compared to as a tool of worth and/or value. If you are one that may need to ditch your comparative measuring stick, here are a few things that you can do to hack it and regain your Godfidence.

- Again, be mindful not to compare the outside persona of others to your inside reality. The one thing we can count on is that everyone has struggles but not everyone advertises them.
- Knowing is half the battle. Know that you have been comparing yourself to others and then note the things that trigger your intrigue. Avoid them.
- If you find yourself influenced by major influencers or celebrities, limit your time on social media. Social media is a wonderful thing in that it keeps us up to speed on pop and current events as well as in touch with distant family and friends. But it can also be an elusive trap. It is best in moderation, with self-awareness and with discipline.
- Money really does not buy happiness. We all want nice material things. Caution against coveting the possessions and means of others to the point of discontentment for what you have. Make goals, not comparisons. Count your blessings and be grateful for what you have while continually striving to be better.
- Clap for your folks. Be genuinely happy for the success of others. You are the CEO of YOU and self-advocacy in your position is important.

Self-advocacy and motivation can coexist with the support of your network and circles. Spread the love. What goes around comes right back around.

Dr. Seuss summed it up well. "Today you are you, that is truer than true. There is no one alive who is you-er than you." Bag the comparative measuring stick. It's outdated. It's childish. It's insecure. Who cares if your hair is or is not long enough, thick enough, curly or straight enough? Who judges whether or not your vocabulary is broad enough, articulate enough, or hip enough? Moreover, who is the judge of whether or not you are worthy, bold, or strong enough? Work on strengthening your own well-being and mental fitness, whatever that means to you. Your focus should be on internal growth, self-kindness, grace, hard work, and resilience. You in comparison to you is an unstoppable force.

# 29

## Doing Well. Good Enough.

*"The longer you perform for someone else's audience, the longer you leave yours hanging."*

-Dr. Shalonda Crawford

Avoid complacency. The trouble with doing well and being "good enough" is that good enough only requires pats on the back and acknowledgments from others to indicate that we are doing a good job. Getting a B- is in general a good job. In many instances it is good enough. But if over the course of the class we settle for B's when our capability better reflects A's, then "doing well" or "good enough" does not properly or effectively serve us.

The real danger in doing good enough is going through our days or weeks performing and executing tasks with excellence and at the same time with no real effort. We have effectively mastered the tasks and so now we are able to do them with ease. So much so that everybody compliments us. We've got this and everyone loves us for it. We have arrived. But have we though? If we are constantly hearing, *"Well done!"* but have not done anything that pushes us out of your comfort zone, we are not on a trajectory that will propel us to a better version of ourselves. We are not operating as the most effective CEO for our organizations that we can be. Essentially, employing complacency is not good for business.

We are human. We all reach lulls when we feel stuck, uncreative, hindered, or at a contemplative crossroad. These mental junctures are also a part of the human experience. They are temporary. Just as we have successfully endured in the past, we too will endure again. When we feel capped by our own capacity, we should reach in and employ our DAs and those in the inner circle. Why be decent when you are actually great?

*Does Decent Fly, or Do I?*

Finally. After several years traversing the academia of a clinical psychology incline, I eventually landed on the back side of that mountain. Surely, it has to be downhill from here. I secured the pre-doc internship of my choice at a community mental health clinic for children. I found myself eager and ready to take on the challenge that I'd signed up for. I completed 800 practicum hours and the last classes required were officially in the bag when I excitedly entered into what I would later learn to be the most arduous phase of my young career.

Gambling on the best investment for my future, I'd turned down two other paid internships for this one. I prayed, *"Lord, can we make a deal? If I work this unpaid internship to the best of my ability—giving my all as if I'm being paid my worth, will you hook me up on the next job opportunity?"* I closed that prayer on that day with a good feeling and definitely up for my new pact with God and for my part of the challenge that came along with it.

Day 1 of my one-year contract at the children's clinic was entered and conquered with the interest and enthusiasm of my own inner child. Day in and day out. I felt more and more accomplished as the pages of the calendar flipped and as I drew deeper in the hands-on experience and niche opportunities that the work afforded me. As my client care and caseload became increasingly more critical, so too did my confidence, as the immediate supervisor was never short of accolades and pats on the back. For the first time in my life, I felt a sense of accomplishment in the professional arena. Each day, I found myself coasting into the clinic ready to change and effect lives one child at a time, one parent at a time, and ultimately one family at time. I was flying high on Cloud 9. Until the day I crashed.

The year was rounding up on a typically overcast December day in Los Angeles. I arrived at the clinic and began to hunker down on my administrative duties as per usual. But on that day though, I was called into an unscheduled meeting. An intrusive departure from my regularly scheduled regimen. Something was definitely awry. My brain scrambled and sifted through the Rolodex of my mind vigorously trying to find any issue with the most recent client interactions, assessments, and documentation that may be at fault. Nothing. I had only given my best, so I could not fathom what could be so wrong.

It turns out, I wasn't so wrong after all. My supervisor failed to provide me a very crucial training on a mandatory assessment tool and a state audit was just days away. *She* was under fire for that oversight and so she decided that *I* would share the brunt of the scolding. From that point on everything changed. Effective immediately, I became her whipping post. Away with the attaboys and in with the antagonizing. Welcomed critical feedback became dreaded captious faultfinding with little to no guidance and supervision. I could do nothing right. I was assigned clients with levels of care beyond my experience. And when I inevitably struggled, I could only find empathy in my fellow internmates. The three of them had been my firsthand witnesses and understood like no one else could. Naturally, I found solace in their comfort. I was grateful for them, but I fought hard to hang on to the confidence I'd built and to the promise I'd made with God. At that time, I had four very long months to go.

The contemptuous crossroad had zoomed full screen into view. From where I was standing, in my tormented mind's eye, I had 3 simple, but not really so simple choices: (1) Leave. But leaving would cause me to breech my contract and risk graduation. (2) Stay, do the very minimum required each day and go home. But that mediocrity would negatively and directly impact the clients I'd been assigned to. After all, I cared deeply about their welfare. (3) Honor my pact with God. Stay and give my very best as if I was getting paid my worth.

Though better is best, I was ultimately faced with the choice to do well or to merely do good enough. I was tested daily. I felt like I was in a war with myself. At the end of each workday, I felt spiritually, mentally, and emotionally battered, bruised, and fatigued. As I rounded the corner and entered the parking lot each morning, I was already overwhelmed and daunted before I exited my car and entered the building. Those were tough days. Nevertheless, at the end of the contract, I chose well (Option 3), and God showed out. In this case, my doing well was good enough.

# 30

# Minefield Mindsets

*"I will not allow anyone to walk in my mind with dirty feet."*

-Gandhi

I t is true that mindsets move mental mountains. Both success and failure rest in the mindset that is chosen at the start of a task. Do you believe you can? Do you expect that you will? Expectation sits in the mindset driver's seat and worldview is its cozy companion coasting along in the passenger seat. The minefield mindset is a mental state that is vigilantly focused on the potential fears and negative outcomes that life *may* throw your way.

You typically get what you expect. When you lead with expectation, your worldview seeks to confirm what you expect. Said another way, when you expect the worst, subconsciously, you filter out the positives and illuminate the negatives in your environment. Minefield mindsets tend to magnify nonconstructive probabilities and pressures while simultaneously blocking out affirmative experiences and happenstances. Negative filtering distorts perceptions and ultimately causes self-sabotage by navigating life through a blurred lens and skewed expectations. If you go to bed Sunday night dreading Monday morning, you are more likely to wake up sluggish, apathetic, grouchy, off-putting, and apt to have a long and challenged Monday.

There are, still, a few mindsets that can cause a mental bind leading to an explosion of stuckness. A fixed, rigid, or bull-headed mindset is most likely to give up in the face of adversity largely because of the dogmatic belief that there are only a few narrow ways of going about reaching success. If you are not careful, minefield mindsets can lead you down the road to challenges that hinder personal success, growth, well-being, and an overall sense of contentment. Discontentment strains relationships. Minefield mindsets breakdown trust, vulnerability, and genuinely intimate connections with others. It is near impossible to forge healthy relationships with negativity constant leading the way.

Lastly, over time, minefield mindsets prevent you from becoming your best you. Self-limiting beliefs and expectations only reinforce its own ideas. This mentality will undoubtedly and eventually hold you back from not only reaching your full potential but moreover prevent you from even attempting your full potential, resulting in you falling short of your dreams and goals as opposed to pursing and reaching them.

# 31

## Cocky Confidence

*"Speak your truth and then listen to it."*

-Dr. Shalonda Crawford

C ocky Confidence is on the other end of the Minefield Mindset spectrum. While there is absolutely nothing wrong with being confident about who we are, what we have to offer the world, and how we present ourselves in a given scenario, cockiness should be cautioned. When confidence slides over into cockiness, it repels, alienates, and ultimately builds a barrier between us and the winning social and professional team that we need and desire. Developing a healthy sense of self is essential for success and allows people to believe in our abilities to lead and defeat challenges.

Conceit or cocky on the other hand is anchored and takes root in a deep lack of self-awareness and misconception. A conceited person believes things that are not innately true, i.e., they are better than others, are entitled to preferential attention, treatment, and opportunities. On top of that, they have a propensity to be rude, selfish, inconsiderate, and unkind to those they deem beneath them. A number of different factors can contribute to cocky-confidence. Environmental factors greatly impact or determine conceit and confidence: upbringing, culture, personality, and past experiences.

Confidence that is backed by a valid and proven track record is not inherently a bad thing. It is overconfidence and cocky-confidence that gets in the way, particularly when we fail to deliver on what we sold. If we are honest, we are all at the center of our own universes, as we should be. Little in our worlds is achieved without our involvement. Imagine the weight of influence that our lived experiences have on our worldviews and self-perceptions. It is not surprising that our thoughts, needs, wants, desires, and dreams loom at the forefront of our minds and the motivation of our lives.

Were you confirmed or denied in your most important efforts? The answer to that question is often at the foundation of either conceit or confidence. Those who are denied validation at pivotal points in life tend to form an over-exaggerated sense of self that masks deep-seated insecurity, while those who are encouraged and cheered gain a healthy sense of confidence in response. Those who experienced critical feedback with love and genuine consideration tend to develop confidence from that feedback, whereas those who are merely offered harsh criticism tend to struggle with self-esteem and even self-love.

# 32

## Indecision Decides

*"Faith as a noun is easy. Faith as a verb... not so much."*

-Dr. Shalonda Crawford

The inability to decide actually is a decision. By not making the choice, the choice is inevitably made. Do not find yourself stuck in a pattern of endless second-guessing and looming anticipation. You are blowing in the wind my friend. You are in the driver's seat, you have taken your hands off the wheel, and you are allowing the car's alignment to navigate your trip. You are going wherever your car decides. How safe do you feel? Not safe at all. The fear of making the wrong decision or making a mistake is typically at hand. The bigger problem though is that indecisiveness leads to missed opportunities. It is simple. Stalling out, prolonging, and putting off making a decision essentially leaves you swaying in the balance and results that are up to chance and circumstance.

Procrastination is putting yourself last. Many of my colleagues agree that procrastination is a self-defeating behavior that is marked by short-term benefits and long-term costs. When we count those costs, putting things off usually and inadvertently causes an unhelpful impact our ability to produce our own expected results independently and individually. We often fall into this temptress trap when faced with serious dilemmas that involve interpersonal relationships, medical, health, or financial issues. Procrastination is avoidance at its best. Avoidance can lead to more stress, and increased stress can perpetuate a cycle of preventable poor physical, emotional, and mental health. We may also put things off out of fear. Fear of self-efficacy, embarrassment, judgment of others, and perfectionism can be terrorizing paralyzers.

When we procrastinate, we risk being totally susceptible to whatever comes our way and preventable undesired results. We forfeit our power to change, effect, and influence the situation or event before us. For every action or nonaction, there is an equal and opposite reaction. Delaying your verdict will not magically make things happen or make them easier later. In fact, a delayed response often makes things even worse.

Developing the habit of procrastination is a sure pitfall. On both major and minor scales, I have personally found myself in the grips of prolonged adjournment, which has led to the pain of procrastination more times than I would like to admit. And I am not alone. We all procrastinate from time to time. According to a 2014 study on procrastination and coping, 20–25% of adults worldwide are chronic procrastinators.[13] Procrastination actually can be an indicator of larger mental health concerns and is connected to overall negative functioning. Our minds have a natural propensity to move into unhelpful and nonconstructive thinking. When faced with scary possibilities or when faced with two unfavorable results, we lean into avoidance because we are afraid to face the doom and gloom of the possibilities. Here are a few to caution:

- Stagnation and stuckness
- Inaction perpetuates a sense of idleness and hence an inability to move forward
- Prevents us from making necessary life changes
- Missed opportunities
- Missing out on chances for enjoyment, relief, and personal growth
- Missing out on professional and vocational advancements and promotions
- Diminished confidence
- Undermines autonomy and the sense of self-efficacy
- Shrinks self-belief.

If any of this hit home, take back your power before you fall prey to paralysis and the inability to make a decision at all. Here's how you do it:

- If it's too big, break it down.
- See the big picture *and* the immediate picture.
- You have a 5-year plan. Great. What do you need to do in Year 1 to accomplish the plan? Year 2? 3, 4 and finally Year 5?
- Get organized.
- Make a "to-do" list and prioritize it.
- Schedule tasks and projects.
- Set time-bound goals.
- Error track—Keep note of things that are not working. It is always good to know what you're doing wrong so that you can dump ineffective models. It is equally important to track the things that are going and doing good as well.
- Just do it!
- Bet on yourself. Throw fear to the wind and fall into it.

# VII

# Part VII: The Interview & Evaluation

*"A job interview is not a test of your knowledge but your ability to use it at the right time."*

*-Unknown*

# 33

## Put Your Best Foot Forward

*"Focus more on your own actions and intentions and less on the validations of others."*

-Dr. Shalonda Crawford

Motivation and determination are gifts of God. "Putting your best foot forward," is a common expression used to indicate making the best impression by presenting yourself in the best possible light. We all want to appear at our absolute best, right? Well then why are we so apprehensive about doing so? I would venture to guess that there is something tucked away in our backpacks of life that is psychologically weighing us down. Trauma can have a significant and impairing effect on why we may be reluctant to be shone in our best lights as well as the hue of light we choose to be shown in. Those traumatic bricks in our backpacks are likely the culprit holding us back in various aspects of life. Haven't we all encountered those times when we have the skill, talent, preparedness, and competence, but still nervous about taking the next step, going for the position, or making the move? Why is confidence not stepping up to the plate in the clutch of the game? Here are a few psychological thought patterns that are rooted in past trauma that hinder our ability to present in the best possible way.

The number one confidence perpetrator is *fear.* More specifically, the fear of failure, the fear of making mistakes, of missing the mark, of being judged, and of falling short of the expectation can all dampen our self-reliance and assertiveness. Bricks of trauma can cause fear and hypervigilance that make it tough to feel safe and secure enough internally to present confidently in spaces that are not promising or favorable. Painful past experiences can also erode our self-esteem and/or self-worth. Impaired *self-esteem* is one of the heaviest bricks that can cause back-breaking negative self-perceptions and beliefs that also hinder confidence. And, unfortunately, when we do not believe that we can prevail, it is all the more difficult to showcase our abilities with the conviction needed to move to the next step. Which means that we essentially do not have much trust in our own abilities. Why? Because unaddressed trauma can impact our ability to trust others, but, most detrimentally, it can cause us to mistrust ourselves. That *lack of trust* may even hinder the willingness to seek or advocate for help from others to guide us or improve our presentations more favorably.

Digging a bit further into the backpack, we may find that as a result of unhealthy and painful relationships, our social interactions may also present challenges that make it difficult to navigate in the most optimal light when it is important to do so. As a result, what commonly follows is *emotional dysregulation.* Traumatic experiences can cause us to find it hard to manage our emotions. When under pressure, instead of the cool, calm, and collective thinking that we wish to employ, we manifest anxiety, mood swings, frustration, outbursts, and even emotional shutdowns. All of which interfere with the required composed and confident presentation that we desire. If this is the case too many times, we are apt to employ *avoidance tactics*. Substances like drugs and alcohol act as an ego-booster or an escape from the discomfort of the experience or memory. Daydreaming and fleeting thoughts, shying away from eye contact or low speaking tones are just a few examples of behaviors we hire to avoid the pressure of putting our best efforts up front. And last, but certainly not least, *negative self-talk*. That pesty and unfavorable internal dialogue can be another one of our self-limiting liabilities. We all tend to engage in negative self-talk from time to time. Though it too has its pros and cons, it primarily does not work in our favor. In my pointed observation of people in general over time, I have noted that most of us naturally lean into the worst-case scenarios when faced with what we perceive as momentous feats. It's not always a bad thing. If we are prepared for the worst, well . . . it's only up from there, right? Yeah, but not when we ruminate on things to the point of detriment. Particularly when past traumatic experiences are triggered. Trauma can act as a reinforcer of inadequacy and unworthiness that can, if not confronted, prevent us from showcasing the greatness we have to offer.

Here again is yet another reason to confront and resolve painful experiences. When we do not, they chop off our best efforts and hold our opportunities hostage. Confronting psychological and emotional trauma, not only assists in life overall, but in overcoming barriers that prevent us from placing our best feet, one before the other, and heading toward extending ourselves in the most optimal, constructive, and assertive brilliance.

Not until we do the necessary work to remove psychological barriers and gain mastery over emotional spiritual and emotional hindrances, are we ready to emerge on the scene. Then, putting your best foot forward can express its potential and its key values. Now, we can make positive and memorable impressions and place our skills, professionalism, and personalities on display. We can enhance and capitalize on opportunities when they come knocking. Experiencing the positive results of being in our best lights will drive motivation and determination and will fuel the desire for excellence in passionate and meaningful endeavors. In that space we close deals and nurture relationships with confidence and full esteem. Personal growth will always include putting your best foot forward. Achieving subjective success inadvertently increases the odds of reaching projected goals and closing pursued deals. Now . . . walk it out!

# 34

## An Effective Resume

*"You are the only you. You are uniquely your own superpower."*

*-Dr. Shalonda Crawford*

G reatness matches every outfit.
We are aware of the pitfalls. Now it's time to shine. The resume's job is to present you in the very best light. An effective resume highlights your strengths and lists your qualifications and relevant past positions, titles, and roles. We now fully understand the role and significance that each of our experiences have played in our lives and how to leverage them to the best of our abilities. We know concretely that every experience is preparation for an experience to come. Because we understand this concept, we will better appreciate the uncomfortable and hurtful involvements that we encounter. It is inside of those very experiences that we have been prepared for the experiences to come alongside the journey ahead. It never stops. As long as we are progressing forward in life, we are also being prepared

for our next encounters.

As we review our past experiences, we should be mindful to be kind to ourselves. Giving ourselves the same grace and understanding that we extend to others and that we effectively deserve. In the same manner that we don't judge or want to be judged, we should also make a pointed effort not to judge ourselves. We have been through the fire. As a result of fire, we are being refined, molded, and shaped into greatness. Extend patience to yourself.

Never forget your fire. We know what it is like to be in the furnace of life. We fully understand the toughness required to endure it, so we should extend our expertise to others who are trying to make their way through as well. When you show up to serve up and present what you have to offer to the world, your presentation should embody all of that greatness.

# 35

# Retention and Development

*"One can choose to go back toward safety or forward toward growth. Growth must be chosen again and again; fear must be overcome again and again."*

*- Abraham Maslow*

H ang on.

The gift makes room for you. Honing the gift keeps you in the room. We are all born with innate instincts and natural gifts. All of us. But not every one of us will use them to our greatest potential. We are all shining stars. But not all of us shine brightly. For that reason, it is the brightest stars that bend ears and illuminate rooms. Intrinsic magnetism may be enough to pull us in advantageous directions, with promising people, and to the tables that are beneficial. But now that we have found and earned our seat at the table, how do we prevent losing it to the next eager beaver vying for our spot? Great wondering. We do this by keeping our best foot in front and intentionally remaining at the head of the game, proactively pursuing ways to improve and develop as individuals and expound upon our gifts.

The essence of the Proverbs 18:16[14] Bible verse, "a person's gifts will bring them before great people," can be interpreted to mean that when we intentionally exercise our God-given gifts, the world opens up to receive us and employs us for them. Just as there is a pay range for a posted employment offering, so there is for our gifts. The value of our offering determines the compensation. That compensation may come in various forms of payment, like opportunities, exposure, relationships, money, advantage, and favor, etc., all with residual potential. Essentially, the gift that is you, will enable you to accomplish your discovered dreams and visions. Further, it will make a pathway to success and fulfillment, divine purpose, and meaning in our lives.

Finally, it is not enough to employ your pain and put it to work for you. Merely retaining a position is the first step but is still just not enough. There is no return on a stagnant investment. We must make a conscientious and industrious effort to continually develop it and to pay it forward to others of whom may also benefit from it. That is how every good investment is multiplied. Break free from the stingy, me-me-me attitude and find your village. Share with your employment pool.

# 36

# Networking

With the notion that our healing is contingent upon our willingness and effort to heal others at the forefront of thought, finding our employment pool becomes vitally key, not only for ourselves but also for others who are in need of our experiential expertise. Because we are "employing our pain," we are to remain cognizant about what and who we hire on to our life missions and bottom lines moving forward. There are a few ways to go about discovering those who need what we have to offer and how we may locate and engage them. First, define and identify who they are. Now that we have examined our current and past pain and trauma, which have consequentially led us to enlightenment, passion, and mission, we can now narrow down our pools of prospects to those that align with that.

Several years ago, I encountered a man, who we will call Chris. Chris spent much of his young adult life homeless. During his initial therapy session, he shared with me that he, his father, and 3 younger siblings spent many days hustling for food to eat, adequate clothing for the four-seasoned climate of the east coast, and many nights on various couches, in vehicles, and low-budget hotel rooms. As his story goes, Chris and all of his family were eventually able to overcome and not permanently succumb to that lifestyle. Nevertheless, that experience, with all of its pros and cons, will always be with him. As he reflected in session, he understands now how fortunate he is to be on the victorious side of that chapter of his life. More importantly, he was also able to identify how having to survive under those conditions have in many regards shaped, fortified, and equipped him in ways that would not have otherwise been possible.

As we processed through those and other tough events, Chris was vividly able to recall the mental pain and practical discomfort of his reality during those times. As if reliving the moments, in real time he recalled being further pained by the judgment of others that he and his family were met with during times when what they needed and immensely longed for was assistance and an extension of human compassion.

Today, Chris undoubtedly knows who he is assigned to help. And, no matter which city he enters, he knows how to find his pool of folks to aid and assist. Furthermore, he is an expert in navigating and surviving life on the streets. He dedicates his life to helping others find their maps and ways out. He helps them place their feet on stable ground and links them to mental, medical, educational, spiritual, and financial resources. Chris makes a point to network by placing himself in spaces where his personal experiences and resources are needed, sought, and most gratifyingly appreciated.

# VIII

# Part VIII: Who's the Boss?

*When I walk through the door, I feel one with the room.*
*-Dr. Shalonda Crawford*

# 37

# Who's In Charge?

*"Success doesn't come from what you do occasionally. It comes from what you do consistently."*

-Marie Forleo

T *he CEO of ME*
So, who's in charge here? You or your pain? Well, from where I sit, YOU are the CEO of YOU. When I say EMPLOY YOUR PAIN—if pain is going to be a companion in your life, make it make "purpose cents." If pain is going to take up space in your life—instead of paying *it* rent, it's even better yet if you put it to work for you. If pain is going to be there, by no choice or doing of your own, make it work for you. It should be bringing you gain just as much as it brought you pain. Make it check in. You're a boss. You're the CEO of your brand. You're the CEO of your life. You are the person in control. You are the person making the decisions. You are the engine behind you; of course, God is the ultimate authority but . . . no one else has control over your life

unless you give them that power. Always hang on to that.

You are the CEO of your life. Everything that is happening in your life should be working for you—and that especially and most primarily includes your pain. So, your story will or should end with how this pain is a part of the evolution into who you are destined to be. There are entire foundations that have been created as a result of someone's pain. Research pushed forward because of someone's pain. I lost my brother to a drunk driver years ago. I have benefited from and I am grateful for the efforts and passion of the mother who lost her child to a drunk driver because her painful experience led her to start MADD, Mothers Against Drunk Drivers. Let's look at the pain of those who suffer from mental health conditions. So many pendulums have been pushed forward in the areas of education and awareness with diagnoses like autism, schizophrenia, even depression and anxiety because of someone's pain. Out of the heartache and the struggle of family members of people with mental health diagnoses to find adequate support and resources to help their loved ones came organizations like NAMI, the National Alliance on Mental Illness. As Black people, we can be grateful for the pain that the founders of the Civil Rights movement endured and the efforts that went forth as a result of it. It's what we *do* with the pain. How are you working your pain? Does your life reflect and somehow benefit, not just you but anyone else in your proximity?

Your pain actually points to your future. Do you realize that your *pain* is what has you bothered by things that don't bother other people? Sometimes we can get mad at people when they are not as passionate about problems that we are passionate about. Well guess what? Your passion is usually stirred up by some type of event or happening that you experienced that caused those feelings that you feel. You're all like, *That doesn't make you mad? That doesn't make you upset? You don't care about that?* What makes you upset is influenced and charged up by experiences. Your worldview is the result. Other folks also have their own experiences, worldview, and things that they are passionate about. You may find out that you care about a certain group of people or a cause or root for an underdog *because* of what was done to you. And here you are ruminating and trying to figure out why you're so passionate about it. It's really important for you to make this all connect.

Making friends has proven to be a challenge but making associates comes easy. I've always been an active and social person. As the old adage goes, "I've never met a stranger." And to add to that, in recent times, I haven't taken on a challenge without an intent determination to conquer it. Break out of your shell. From today forward, when you wake up in the morning it's, "Hello World. Here I come!"

# 38

# Shed the Shell

*"If the cost is your peace of mind, it's too expensive."*

*-Dr. Shalonda Crawford*

R elease and exhale. Feeling sorry for yourself is not always pitiful. As a matter of fact, *"feeling"* for yourself is being immensely sympathetic toward self. Feeling sorry for myself is only problematic when I lack self-awareness about it or when I am unwilling to take ownership and accountability and make the necessary changes. Contrarily, feeling for ourselves, even when what we feel is sorrow, is an extension of grace to self. It is actually doing something positive for self and is ultimately providing the inner self with what it desires to extend to others but more importantly, to receive for itself. We all want to be seen, heard, recognized, and noticed for who we are authentically. Acceptance is at the root of healing. Acknowledgment of the importance of our existence in the world is the starting place for empowerment. What if we could do that for ourselves? Oh, but we can!

Shed the shell. Abandon the tough guy costume. There was a time when the hardcore exterior and public-facing face served a purpose, but that time has passed. We destroy our own psyches with reckless abandon by judging ourselves, shaming ourselves, not advocating for ourselves, being overly critical of ourselves, negatively talking ourselves out of profitable opportunities, accomplishments, goals, and states of mind. Sometimes we are deeply injured because others will not attempt to extend a kind hand to reach out us. And yet we abandon ourselves when we don't recognize our own pain. We cheat ourselves when we will not or cannot sit in our own pain. We prolong the healing process when we are not compassionate about our pained places.

Have you ever had a person connect with you and speak to you with with a soft and kind and loving tone? From today forward, let us be mindful not to speak with ourselves in contrast to that example. Let us be better about improving our internal conversations. Tough love is good and harsh conversations are also necessary. But gentle conversations with self are the launching pad to intimacy with self and external connections with others in your circles and networks. In this way, we model how we want to feel and be interacted with.

At the core of us there is a real person in there that is immensely kind and loving. There is a bright light that yearns to illuminate our worlds and those that encounter it. There is a sweet, sweet voice that belongs solely to us, but it is also the hardest voice to hear and locate. We cannot abandon the search to project and amplify it. It is uniquely your voice. It is uniquely mine. But in order to be heard and/or seen, we have to continue to move past the fear, shed the excess baggage, break out of our shells, and grow.

Blossom. Bloom unapologetically. It is scary to navigate life lightly and freely without the need to defend who we are but to simply be who we are. So make the decision today. Embrace the painful past. Prepare for the pain that will inevitably come. Shed the shell. And, live!

# Epilogue

*"Share love and laughter unapologetically without being hushed."*

-Dr. Shalonda Crawford

## Purpose Cents

The goal has not been to usher you into a therapy session but rather to share my thoughts and human experiences with you. Through the ups and downs, and the joys and pains of it all, I now know that love is our greatest asset. It is a powerful tool. It is a guiding light. It is the most dangerous weapon. It is the gentlest comforter. It is the solid and infallible foundation. Love is the ultimate acceptance. Although we fall and fail, we are all purposed to love.

In summation, throughout the course of my life, I've learned that pain makes purpose make perfect sense. It makes purpose-sense. I cannot expect a return on an investment that I have yet to make. Dividends follow life's painful experiences. It gets better after it's been worse or gets worse before it's over. It's not our circumstances that dictate our reality. It's our own perspectives that navigate our existence. All of the pain that we have ever endured stands to reason equivalent or proportionate positive payback. I've figured out how to turn disadvantages into advantages. I've learned to how to allow my most painful experiences to be the source of inspiration, not just for myself but more importantly for others. I know that tension has the potential to produce the real progress needed for my own reform and it will, when and if properly directed, motivate me to action. When it's all said and done, it just makes purpose cents.

# Key Words

**Acceptance** - the ultimate goal of the grief process leading to healing, wholeness, renewal and acceptance of loss.

**Acute Trauma** - typically results from a single and isolated incident, like a physical altercation, a serious injury, or a car accident.

**Avoidance Tactic** - a mental escape from the discomfort of an experience or memory, i.e. daydreaming, fleeting thoughts, shying away from eye contact or low speaking tones, procrastination, addiction, etc.

**Being** - the essence of who one is at the inner core.

**Best Foot Forward** - a common expression used to indicate making the best impression by presenting yourself in the best possible light.

**Bricks in the Backpack** - unhealed and therefore unresolved trauma and painful events and experiences of life.

**Cargo Pants** - a metaphor that describes the categorization of people in the life circle and further, where to place them.

**Chronic Trauma** - typically happens when the event is repeated and prolonged like, homelessness, domestic violence, or chronic illnesses.

**Cocky Confidence** - a mindset that repels, alienates, and ultimately builds a barrier between self and the inner needs and desires.

**Comparative Measuring Stick** - a means of determining personal status, value, and/or requirements for yourself in contrast to others.

**Complex Trauma** - exposure to varied and multiple traumatic events, usually of an invasive and/or interpersonal nature.

**DABDA** - describes the stages of grief. DABDA stands for Denial, Anger, Bargaining, Depression and Acceptance.

**Determination Advocates** - accountability partners to keep us grounded, responsible and operating towards purpose and in our uniqueness.

**Desert Season** - healthy isolation; withdrawal and retreat into personal solidarity.

**Doing** - supposes the actions that we take, the behaviors we employ, and the choices we actually make.

**Empathy** - joining with someone to embrace their experience as much as you can imagine having the experience yourself.

**Emotional Dysregulation** – characterized by the difficulty to control emotions and thus behaviors.

**Failing Backwards** - neglect to take inventory or reflect and then continue to make the same mistakes repeatedly while genuinely believing that things will change or be different.

**Forgiveness** - a personal and intentional decision to enter the process of releasing anger and/or resentment.

**Godfidence** - embracing the confidence that God has in you; leaning into His understanding of you.

**Meta Thinking** - thinking about the way one thinks and understanding the patterns behind the thought patterns.

**Minefield Mindset**s - a mental state that is vigilantly focused on the potential fears and negative outcomes that one may encounter.

**Negative Self-talk** – a pessimistic, antagonistic and critical inner voice that erodes confidence.

**Networking** - establishing your employment pool and making pointed effort to engage in spaces where personal experiences and resources are needed, sought and most gratifyingly appreciated.

**Pain** - the gatekeeper. A security guard. Pain serves a useful and important purpose. The intention of pain is to prevent and warn us from becoming more injured.

**Passion** - the incitement to do what is within our reach and capabilities.

**Paying It Forward** - describes the beneficiary of a good deed, repaying that same sentiment of kindness to another or others rather than paying it back to self.

**Personal Exceptionalism** - a common struggle for people trying to find stability from forms of addiction. *see also Terminal Uniqueness*

**Processing** - the method of focusing, digesting and integrating a person's thoughts, feelings, and experiences in response to an event.

**Purpose** - the plan for our lives that God has orchestrated.

**Regret** - our mind's attempt to reconcile disappointment.

**Repression** - a subconscious, unhealthy, powerful psychological defense for survival and a sense of normalcy.

**Resilience** - mental toughness required to adapt to trauma, life challenges, adversity and other presented stressors.

**Self-esteem** - belief about self-worth, respect and abilities.

**Self-sabotage** - anything that we do to hinder or prevent our own forward progression towards success or recovery.

**Suppression** – a voluntary, more healthy coping mechanism that allows us to block painful experiences from awareness until there is a better time to respond.

**Steward** - the manager of opportunities and experiences entrusted in our care.

**Sympathy** - the act of being present and open to the experiences of others.

**Terminal Uniqueness** - the idea that an experience is so vastly special or different from anyone else's that the person alone has uniquely experienced or is experiencing it. *see also Personal Exceptionalism*

**Trauma** - what happens *inside* you as a result of what happened *to* you.

**Toxic Forgiveness** - a mechanism used to *avoid* conflict and settle difficult or unresolved feelings and thoughts, but betrays self because it masks true feelings.

**Unforgiveness** - unwillingness or resistance to make allowances for mistakes or extend forgiveness for past hurts or offenses.

**Void** – It is an empty place in your psyche that is created by actively or subconsciously dodging problems.

# Notes

PAIN + PASSION = PURPOSE

1   Warren, R. (2002). *The Purpose Driven Life.* Zondervan.

TRAUMA

2   *Maté, G., & Maté, D. (2022). The myth of normal: trauma, illness & healing in a toxic culture.* New York, Avery, an imprint of Penguin Random House.

3   *How early childhood trauma is unique.* (2023, June 7). The National ChildTraumatic Stress Network.https://www.nctsn.org/what-is-child-trauma/trauma-types/early-childhoodtrauma/effects#:~:text=Young%20children%20are%20less%20able,effects%20of%20exposure%20to%20trauma

GETTING ON WITH LIFE

4   (2023, April 25). National Student Clearing House. https://www.studentclearinghouse.org/news/college-student-stop-out-population-increased-3-6-from-previous-year/

THE REWARD OF RESILIENCE

5   American Psychological Association. *The road to resilience.* Washington, DC: American Psychological Association; 2014. http://www.apa.org/helpcenter/road-resilience.aspx.

THE CEO OF ME

6   *Good News Translation Bible.* (nd). Bible Hub. https://biblehub.com/habakkuk/2-2.htm

7   Hill, N. (1983). *Think and grow rich.* First Ballantine Books ed. New York, Fawcett Crest

UNHEALED WOUNDS

8   Substance Abuse and Mental Health Services Association. *Coping Tips for Traumatic Events and Disasters.* Substance Abuse and Mental Health Services. Retrieved April 24, 2024, from https://www.samhsa.gov/find-help/disaster-distress-helpline/coping-tips.

9   American Psychological Association. (2023, October 17). *How to cope with traumatic*

*stress: Psychologists recommend people lean on loved ones, prioritize self-care, and be patient with themselves to help manage the stressful effects of trauma.* American Psychological Association. Retrieved November 11, 2024 from https://www.apa.org/t opics/trauma/stress#:~:text=Do%20your%20best%20to%20eat,thinking%20about %20a%20traumatic%20event.)

REGRET

10   Roese, N. J., Epstude, K., Fessel, F., Morrison, M., Smallman, R., Summerville, A., . . . Segerstrom, S. (2009). Repetitive regret, depression, and anxiety: findings from a nationally representative survey. *Journal of Social and Clinical*

DESERT SEASONS

11   New International Version. (ND). Psalm 139:14. *"I praise you because I am fearfully and wonderfully made; your works are wonderful, I know that full well. My frame was not hidden from you when I was made in the secret place, when I was woven together in the depths of the earth."*

THE GIFT OF FAILURE

12   Ward, G. (2021, August 14). *7 Remarkable benefits of failure.* Linked In. https://www.lin kedin.com/pulse/7-remarkable-benefits-offailure-greg-ward/

INDECISION DECIDES

13   Ferrai, JR, & Díaz-Morales, JF. (2014, January). *Procrastination and mental health coping: A brief report related to students.* Research Gate. 256475556_Procrastination_ and_mental_health_coping_A_brief_report_related_to_students

RETENTION AND DEVELOPMENT

14   *New International Version.* (nd). Bible Gateway. https://www.biblegateway.com/passa ge/?search=Proverbs%2018&version=NIV